The ACORD Capability Model

David F. Jones
Nationwide Insurance

David Schmitz
Deloitte Consulting, LLP

Nicholas France
ACORD

Mark Orlandi
ACORD

The ACORD Capability Model

David F. Jones, David Schmitz, Nicholas France, and Mark Orlandi

Copyright © 2010 ACORD Corporation.

All rights reserved. No part of this book shall be reproduced, stored in a retrieval system, or transmitted by any means, electronic, mechanical, photocopying, recording or otherwise without written permission from the publisher. No patent liability is assumed with respect to the use of the information contained herein. Although every precaution has been taken in the preparation of this book, the publisher and authors assume no responsibility for errors or omissions, nor is any liability assumed for damages resulting from use of the information contained herein.

This book is sold subject to the condition that it shall not, by way of trade or otherwise, be lent, resold, hired-out, or otherwise circulated without the publisher's prior consent in any form of binding or cover other than that in which it is published and without a similar condition including this condition being imposed on the subsequent purchaser.

Published by: ACORD Corporation

First printing: October, 2010

ISBN-13: 978-0-9768967-3-9

Trademarks
The ACORD name and logo are registered marks of ACORD Corporation. Third party marks are the property of their respective owners.

Warning and Disclaimer
Every effort has been made to make this book as complete and accurate as possible. HOWEVER, THIS BOOK AND THE INFORMATION CONTAINED HEREIN ARE PROVIDED "AS IS", WITHOUT WARRANTY OF ANY KIND, EXPRESS OR IMPLIED, INCLUDING BUT NOT LIMITED TO, THE WARRANTIES OF MERCHANTABILITY, FITNESS FOR A PARTICULAR PURPOSE, ACCURACY, COMPLETENESS, TITLE AND NONINFRINGEMENT OF THIRD PARTY RIGHTS. The authors and the publisher shall have neither liability nor responsibility to any person or entity with respect to any loss or damages arising from the information contained in this book.

Printed in U.S.A.   Release 1

About the Authors

DAVID F. JONES is a Consultant in IT Architecture at Nationwide Insurance, focused on service oriented architecture and data architecture. He has over 30 years of experience in programming, requirements definition, and architecture, primarily in Personal and Commercial Property and Casualty insurance.

DAVID SCHMITZ is a Director at Deloitte Consulting, LLP (Deloitte) focused on technology strategy and implementation in the insurance industry. He has over 25 years of experience that crosses most insurance lines of business including Personal and Commercial Property and Casualty, Life and Annuities, Group (Health and non-Health), Mortgage, Reinsurance, and Retirement Services.

Deloitte refers to one or more of Deloitte Touche Tohmatsu Limited, a UK private company limited by guarantee, and its network of member firms, each of which is a legally separate and independent entity. Please see www.deloitte.com/about for a detailed description of the legal structure of Deloitte Touche Tohmatsu Limited and its member firms. Please see www.deloitte.com/us/about for a detailed description of the legal structure of Deloitte LLP and its subsidiaries.

NICHOLAS FRANCE is a Technical Architect at ACORD involved in the development and support of the ACORD standards for all domains. He is also involved in the development of joint framework solution standards, including Web Services and Security, and the ACORD Standards Framework. Prior to joining ACORD, Nicholas was a Senior Programmer/Analyst for eight years at AIG, involved in the development and support of internal and external web based applications.

MARK ORLANDI is a Senior Business Analyst involved in the development and maintenance of the ACORD Framework. This role leverages his broad experience with ACORD's P&C/Surety Standards (Forms, AL3, XML) as well as areas involving education/training and data mapping. Prior to joining ACORD in 1998, Mark spent 13 years with Westfield Insurance.

Acknowledgements

Special thanks from David F. Jones:

I would like to thank my colleagues at Nationwide who supported my work with the capability model working group, particularly Mainak Patel for numerous discussions on the purpose and content of the model, and Tiffany Gorski and Vijay Gopal for their encouragement and support of my participation.

Special thanks from David Schmitz:

I would like to thank my many colleagues at Deloitte who supported development of the capability models that formed the foundation of our contribution to ACORD, particularly Ted Epps, John Johnsen, Karan Mishra and Vani Oza who made significant contributions to this effort.

Special thanks from Nicholas France:

Thank you to Frank Neugebauer for inviting me to join in on this collaboration. Thanks also to co-authors David Schmitz and David Jones for making this a thoroughly enjoyable and painless process. I would also like to thank my wife Mary Ann and two children, Zachary and Daniella, for being my support and inspiration, helping me become the person I am today.

Special thanks from Mark Orlandi:

Many thanks to those who have shared their skills, experiences, and insights concerning insurance, technology, and people. Thank you Frank Neugebauer and Shane McCullough for your patience and support.

Forward

The Capability Model is one of several facets in the ACORD Framework that offers members a new approach to standards-setting and implementation. We are providing a valuable asset never before offered by ACORD as we enter a new era of model-based application development. Our community's ability to create and maintain the Capability Model makes possible benefits and cost savings for all participants.

There are a broad range of strategic and tactical uses for the Capability Model within an insurance company. A capability model can be one of the foundational components of a holistic architecture methodology. Perhaps the core value of the Capability Model involves improving communication and providing an organizational framework.

The Capability Model is enterprise level, consisting of both core operational business functions (e.g. new business, claims) as well as corporate functions (e.g., technology, accounting) common to all insurers. Ideally, technology improvements are aligned to support the business strategy and the Capability Model can be a key enabler. A common approach is to use the Capability Model to identify target areas in need of change to support the business strategy.

The Capability Model can function as a communication tool and also as an organizational tool. It can assist with organizational alignment and systems development. It can be utilized to support initiatives involving application portfolio strategy/management, systems development, project portfolio management, and mergers and acquisitions. The examples provided in this book cover some of the many ways the Capability Model can be leveraged to support your business and can help improve the effectiveness of your organization.

ACORD is very grateful for the efforts of the working group and for the donations from IBM and Deloitte. As the development of the ACORD Framework continues, interest is growing and we are optimistic concerning future donations.

Contents

About the Authors. i
Acknowledgements ii
Forward iii

1. Overview and Intended Audience 1–1
    Organization of the Book. 1–1
    The Framework Five Facets 1–2

2. Technical Overview 2–5
    Model Output 2–6
        MagicDraw® Version 2–6
        XMI® Version 2–6
        HTML Version 2–7
        Microsoft® Excel®/Adobe® PDF Version 2–8
    Metamodel Information 2–9
    Areas of the Model 2–9
        Summary Conclusion 2–14

3. The Capability Model: What Insurance Companies Do 3–15
    History of the Capability Model 3–16
    Organization of the Model. 3–16
    Getting the Model 3–17

4. What's New in Version 2.0 4–19
New Content in Version 2 of the ACORD Capability Model 4–19
Structural Changes 4–20

5. Top Level Capabilities: An Overview 5–23
How can the model be used by the Industry and ACORD Membership?............... 5–23
The Ten Capabilities 5–24
    Business Management 5–25
    Channel Management 5–26
    Claims 5–27
    Contract Administration 5–28
    Customer Service 5–28
    Enterprise Services 5–29
    Marketing 5–32
    Product 5–33
    Sales 5–33

6. Detailed Overview–Product 6–35
Product Overview 6–35
Functional Decomposition–Product 6–36
    Product Strategy 6–36
    Product Strategy Development 6–37
        Product Research and Analysis 6–37
        Product Planning 6–37
    Product Innovation 6–38
        Product Portfolio Management 6–38
    Product Performance Analysis 6–38
        Product Development 6–38
    Product Design 6–39
        Product Implementation 6–39
Product Process Maps 6–39
    Product Research and Analysis 6–40
        Conduct Product Market Analysis 6–40

Product Innovation.. 6–40
    Recommend Concept.. 6–41
    Analyze Product Feasibility... 6–41
    Forecast Product Performance.. 6–41
    Identify Product Actions.. 6–41
    Examine Legal Impact.. 6–42

Product Design.. 6–42
    Define Product... 6–42
    Develop Actuarial Assumptions....................................... 6–42
    Define Product Investment Strategy................................... 6–43
    Define Investment Options... 6–43
    Define Product Reinsurance Requirements............................ 6–43
    Define Product Underwriting Standards............................... 6–43
    Define Product Performance Criteria.................................. 6–43
    Identify Product Distribution Channels................................ 6–43
    Define Product Training.. 6–43
    Define Needs Analysis Procedures.................................... 6–43
    Define Product Pricing and Rating.................................... 6–44
    Define Product Reserving.. 6–44
    Define Product Marketing.. 6–44

Product Implementation... 6–44
    Conduct Product Prototyping... 6–45
    Produce Product Documentation..................................... 6–45
    Obtain Regulatory Approvals... 6–45
    Determine Product Roll-out... 6–45
    Conduct Product Testing... 6–45
    Deploy Product.. 6–45

7. Capability Model Uses–An Overview 7–47

The Capability Model as a Communication Tool........................... 7–47

The Capability Model as an Organizational Tool........................... 7–48

The Capability Model Decomposition..................................... 7–48

Capability Model Uses–Business Aligned IT Strategy...................... 7–49
    Example... 7–50

Capability Model Uses–Organizational Alignment 7–52
    Examples 7–52
Capability Model Uses–Application Portfolio Strategy/Management 7–54
    Example. 7–54
Capability Model Uses–Systems Development 7–57
    Example. 7–57
Capability Model Uses–Project Portfolio Management 7–58
    Example. 7–59
Capability Model Uses–Mergers and Acquisitions 7–60
    Example. 7–60
Capability Model Uses–Conclusion 7–62

Parting Thoughts 7–62

Overview and Intended Audience

The ACORD Capability Model, in short, describes the **abilities** and **activities** of the insurance industry. As such, it represents the business of insurance from the business user's point of view. The model is a key element in the ACORD Framework, a series of five models (or facets as they are called) that collectively represent different view of the industry.

This book is intended for anyone wanting to learn more about the ACORD Capability Model, especially business analysts who want to build better business processes and inspire innovation within their organizations. There are no special requirements for understanding the content of this book, although some background in insurance is helpful.

Organization of the Book

The book starts off in this chapter by explaining the ACORD Framework as a whole, in order to give you a basis of understanding. In chapter two, Nick France from ACORD explains the technical aspects of the model, including how to get it (for ACORD Members). Chapter three begins the model explanation, provided by David Jones from Nationwide. In chapter four, Dave Schmitz from Deloitte and David Jones explain what's new in version 2.0 (as compared with version 1.0). Chapter five explains the model at the highest level; the top-level capabilities. Chapter six gives you a preview of the model as David Jones explains the Product capability in detail. The detailed model explanation stops there; you may wonder why we don't cover everything. We don't explain the entire model for two reasons: this is a public book and the model is only available to ACORD Members or Framework licensees. The other reason is sheer content; it would have taken a great deal of time to completely cover every element of the model. We conclude with Dave Schmitz explaining how the model can be used in chapter seven.

Collectively, we provide you with not only the conceptual background of the Capability Model, but a concrete sampling of the model and how such models are used in the real world.

The Framework Five Facets

There are five parts, or facets, to the ACORD Framework. Each facet has one or more relationships to the others, and they collectively represent different views of the business of insurance. This combination of deliverables not only makes using ACORD standards easier, but will also open new doors to innovation.

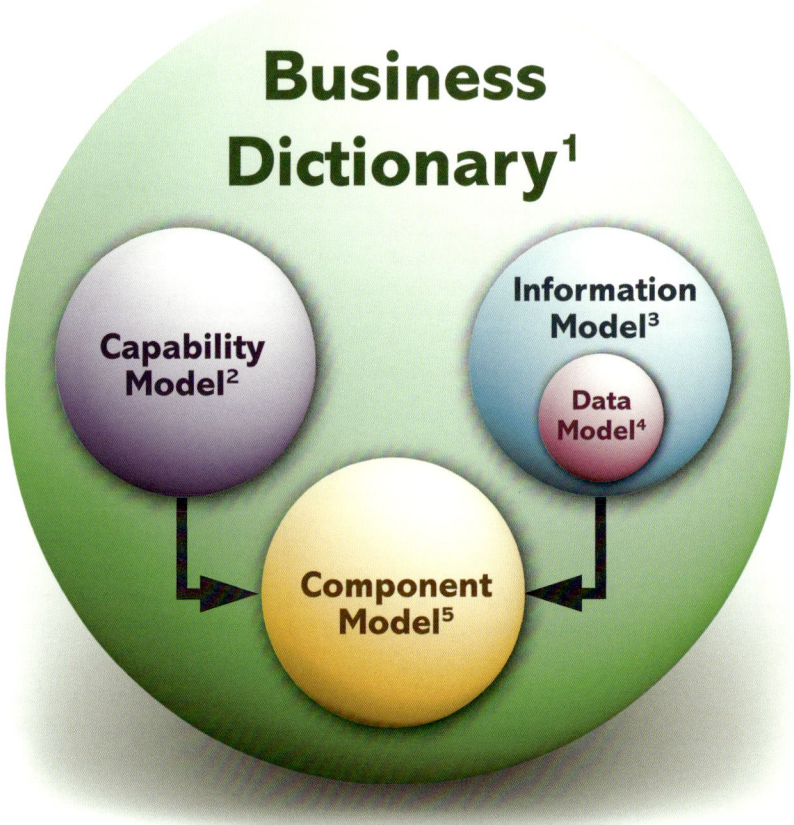

Overview and Intended Audience

1. Business Dictionary—This dictionary is more than just words and their definitions: it consists of insurance concepts (such as "accident location") and includes not only definitions, but synonyms, usage and references within each domain. The dictionary provides the vernacular for the rest of the facets.

The Business Dictionary can be used for everything from project dictionaries to the basis for models like the other facets of the ACORD Framework. The main idea is to aid communication by standardizing the jargon on teams, just as a common language (such as English) can help individuals from different parts of the world communicate.

The terms in the dictionary are harmonized with the other facets of the Framework, ensuring that terms are used synonymously across the models.

2. Capability Model—The Capability Model is the second facet and provides multiple levels of decomposition of the business capabilities down to the level of process (called Process Maps). The capabilities are higher-level and include a functional decomposition in areas such as Claims, Marketing, Product, Business Management and Enterprise Services. The Process Maps expand on the lowest-level capabilities by listing many of the most important processes contained within a given capability. However, those processes do NOT include workflow. Only the names of the processes are given.

The functional and process nature of the ACORD Capability Model allows it to serve as the basis for business process engineering and organization assessment efforts.

3. Information Model—The most detailed facet of the ACORD Framework is the Information Model, which is a conceptual overview of the entire industry. This Unified Modeling Language™ (UML®) model contains a number of functional areas, including Agreement (i.e., policies and non-policy contracts), Product, Party (i.e., people and organizations), and Claims. With almost 900 classes and over 2,300 attributes, this model provides the most granular level of information.

Beyond simply creating an Information Model, ACORD is mapping the current XML, EDI, and forms standards to this model, helping the industry "connect the dots" between ACORD's standards and the insurance content within those standards.

The Information Model has many uses, including a way to gather information requirements and as the basis for programming (e.g., Java, .NET) models and data models.

1–3

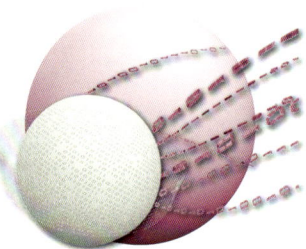

4. Data Model—Since the Information Model can be used to create a data model, ACORD and its membership did just that. The data model–based on the ACORD Working Group definition of the term "data model"–is a logical-level entity-relationship model. This model closely resembles the Information Model but from the data architect's point of view.

There are many uses for this kind of data model, including the basis of a physical model for relational database management systems, the basis of data warehouse models, and the basis of data stores so that they can more easily consume ACORD messages (especially when used with the Information Model as the programming model).

5. Component Model—The fifth and final facet of the ACORD Framework is the Component Model. This model organizes data and behavior into components, allowing separation of the interfaces (which are contained in the model as services) from the implementations of those interfaces. Like the other facets of the Framework, the Component Model is organized around concepts in insurance, including Party, Agreement, and Product (among others). The Component Model contains the logical groupings of components along with service maps, which are the interface definitions (including inputs and outputs) of those components.

This Component Model may have the greatest number of uses, for everything from portfolio rationalization to creating enterprise application architectures.

Now that the background information is out of the way, it's time to learn more about the technical aspects of the model–including how to get it.

Technical Overview

In this chapter I review the technical aspects of the ACORD Capability Model and the tools used to create it. The technical aspects of the model refer to how the model is technically represented, along with information you will need to understand the model. I provide more detail about each area in the "Areas of the Model" section but for now here is an outline of what you can find in the Capability Model.

The ACORD Capability Model was developed using the Unified Modeling Language (UML) and No Magic's MagicDraw® modeling tool. The UML model allows for "profiles," which provide a facility for adding specificity to vanilla UML concepts. The Capability Model has such a UML profile which is used to define a UML shape as a "capability" instead of a vanilla class.

Structurally, the model consists of four layers: the first three layers are capabilities (broken down in a functional decomposition) and the fourth layer is one or more business process "maps." We use the term "process map" because like a roadmap, we give you the points–or activities–without specifying the route–or sequencing. In each of the first three layers of the model there are UML class diagrams, which include properties and associations which help define the relationships. Each item has documentation and additional properties that define that specific area along with its relationships.

To create and update the model, ACORD used No Magic's MagicDraw modeling tool version 16.5. The screenshots and descriptions found in the "Metamodel Information" and "Areas of the Model" sections are taken from this tool. MagicDraw modeling tool is also the application ACORD uses to create multiple output formats, which I describe in the "Model Output" section.

Model Output

The ACORD Capability Model is available for download from the ACORD website (http://www.acord.org/resources/framework/Pages/default.aspx). The model is free for members and available for a fee for non-members. Be sure to log into ACORD.org before you try to download the model.

Once you have downloaded the "ACORD Capability Model 2.0.zip," extract the files using the folder names. The reason for this folder structure is that ACORD publishes the Capability Model in several formats which I will describe in the following sections.

MagicDraw® Version

One of the formats that the model is published in is a MagicDraw .mdkzip file which can be imported only into the MagicDraw modeling tool. ACORD is currently using MagicDraw modeling tool version 16.5 and the files can be found in the ".\ACORD Capability Model 2.0\NoMagic MagicDraw UML" folder from the extract. A free MagicDraw reader can be downloaded from https://secure.nomagic.com/download. You will need to register on the site before being able to download the software. Please select the ACORD Implementation Forum from the heard from drop-down menu when registering. MagicDraw is an award-winning modeling, simulation and analysis solution; providing business process, architecture, systems and software modeling capabilities with teamwork collaboration support. This dynamic and versatile solution facilitates analysis and design of complex systems and systems of systems. MagicDraw is a core component of No Magic's Cameo® Suite. For more information on this modeling solution visit http://www.nomagic.com or http://www.magicdraw.com/download.

XMI® Version

The Unified Modeling Language (UML) is a standardized general-purpose modeling language. The standard is managed by the Object Management Group™ (OMG™). The UML model includes a set of graphical notation techniques to create visual models of business ideas or software-intensive systems. In the context of the Capability Model, it is a visual way to represent a business view of insurance.

The model is also published as an XMI (XML Metadata Interchange) 2.1 file and can be found in the ".\ACORD Capability Model 2.0\XMI-UML Export" folder from the extract. XMI is an OMG standard for exchanging metadata information via Extensible Markup Language (XML) and allows models to be exported and imported between UML modeling tools. The output file is created as an XML file (see figure 2-1) and a third party application can then parse the XML file using standard techniques like DOM or SAX to access the desired data from the UML model. There is no diagram associated with the XMI download since the intent is for you to import it into your UML modeling tool of choice (assuming it supports the XMI format).

```xml
<?xml version='1.0' encoding='UTF-8'?>
<!-- This xmi file is optimized for MagicDraw UML. Some references are not saved. -->
<!-- Change MagicDraw UML environment options property General->.Save Rich XMI -->

<xmi:XMI xmi:version='2.1' xmlns:uml='http://schema.omg.org/spec/UML/2.1.2' xmlns:xmi='http://schema.omg.org/spec/XMI/2.1' xmlns:UML_Standard_Profile='http://www.magicdraw.com/schemas/UML_Standard_Profile.xmi' xmlns:ACORD_Profile='http://www.magicdraw.com/schemas/ACORD_Profile.xmi' xmlns:MagicDraw_Profile='http://www.magicdraw.com/schemas/MagicDraw_Profile.xmi' xmlns:Mapping='http://www.magicdraw.com/schemas/Mapping.xmi' xmlns:DSL_Customization='http://www.magicdraw.com/schemas/DSL_Customization.xmi' xmlns:Data_Type='http://www.magicdraw.com/schemas/Data_Type.xmi' xmlns:Structure='http://www.magicdraw.com/schemas/Structure.xmi' xmlns:Validation_Profile='http://www.magicdraw.com/schemas/Validation_Profile.xmi'>
	<xmi:Documentation exporter='MagicDraw UML' exporterVersion='16.0'/>
	<xmi:Extension extender='MagicDraw UML 16.0' extenderID='MagicDraw UML 16.0'>
		<shareTable shareDescription='IBCS model'>
			<share sharedPackage='_9_5_1_1cb20362_1166784895760_675209_6726'/>
			<share sharedPackage='_9_5_1_1cb20362_1166784895760_600358_6718'/>
		</shareTable>
		<mountTable>
			<module resource='file:/C:/Program%20Files/MagicDraw%20UML%20Community%20Edition/profiles/UML_Standard_Profile.xml' autoloadType='ALWAYS_LOAD' readOnly='true' loadIndex='true' requiredVersion='-1'>
				<mount mountPoint='magicdraw_uml_standard_profile_v_0001' mountedOn='eee_1045467100313_135436_1'/>
			</module>
		</mountTable>
	</xmi:Extension>
	<uml:Model xmi:id='eee_1045467100313_135436_1' name='Data' visibility='public'>
		<packagedElement xmi:type='uml:Package' xmi:id='_9_5_1_1cb20362_1166784895760_675209_6726' name='AF_IM' visibility='public'>
			<xmi:Extension extender='MagicDraw UML 16.0' extenderID='MagicDraw UML 16.0'>
				<moduleExtension moduleRoot='::AF_IM'/>
			</xmi:Extension>
			<ownedComment xmi:type='uml:Comment' xmi:id='_12_5_172302ff_1186664844222_667569_176600' body='ACORD Model'>
				<annotatedElement xmi:idref='_9_5_1_1cb20362_1166784895760_675209_6726'/>
			</ownedComment>
			<packagedElement xmi:type='uml:Package' xmi:id='_16_0_1782030c_1235037303068_637775_34069' name='Business Concepts' visibility='public'>
				<ownedComment xmi:type='uml:Comment' xmi:id='_16_0_1782030c_1235038362370_164484_34092' body='This part of IBCS model contains all domains related to business insurance concept definition.&#10;&#10;It&#39;s been organized in domains structured around Insurance main business concept definition (product, contract, party, claim, etc.).&#10;&#10;These domains have been designed to maximize reuse of business conceptsand follow a strict rule that forbids all circular dependencies.&#10;&#10;'>
					<annotatedElement xmi:idref='_16_0_1782030c_1235037303068_637775_34069'/>
				</ownedComment>
				<packagedElement xmi:type='uml:Package' xmi:id='_9_5_1_1cb20362_1166784895760_95546_6739' name='CTR' visibility='public'>
					<ownedComment xmi:type='uml:Comment' xmi:id='_12_5_172302ff_1186664861767_200627_180047' body='CTR = Contract&#10;This domain models active contracts, their elements and specifications.&#10;&#10;Contract elements and specifications are also used during the underwriting process (to describe the future contract). &#10;&#10;This domain is the main support for Claim management.'>
```

FIGURE 2-1: XMI model representation.

HTML Version

The model is also published as a series of .html files that can be viewed through your web browser. The look and feel of these files is similar to the MagicDraw modeling tool export and can be found in the "\ACORD Capability Model 2.0\HTML" folder from the extract. Double click or open the index.html file to open the model (see figure 2-2).

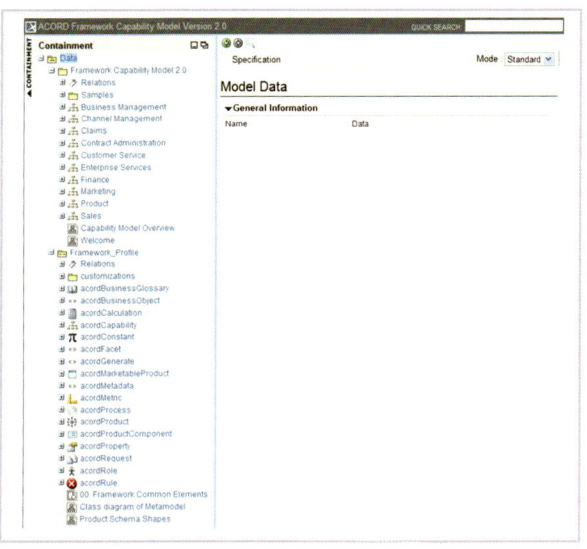

FIGURE 2-2: HTML representation of model.

Microsoft® Excel®/Adobe® PDF Version

Finally, the model is also exported as .xls and .pdf files, which can be found in the ".\ACORD Capability Model 2.0\Spreadsheet" folder from the extract. All three levels of capabilities and process maps and their descriptions can be viewed in a Microsoft Excel spreadsheet or PDF document (see figures 2-3a and 2-3b).

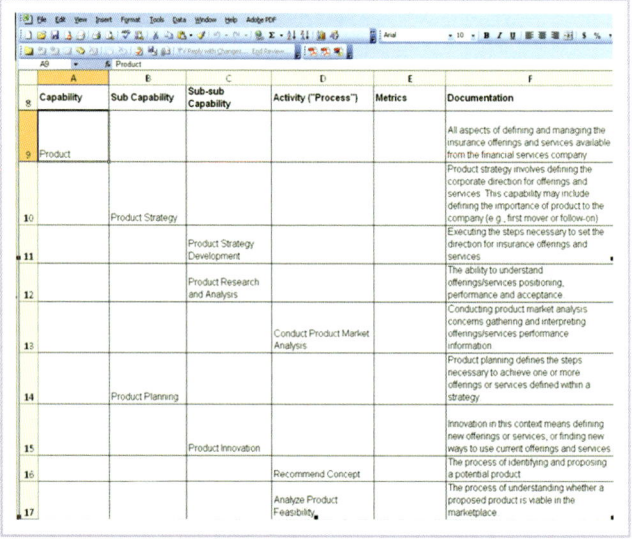

FIGURE 2-3A: Microsoft Excel spreadsheet representation of model.

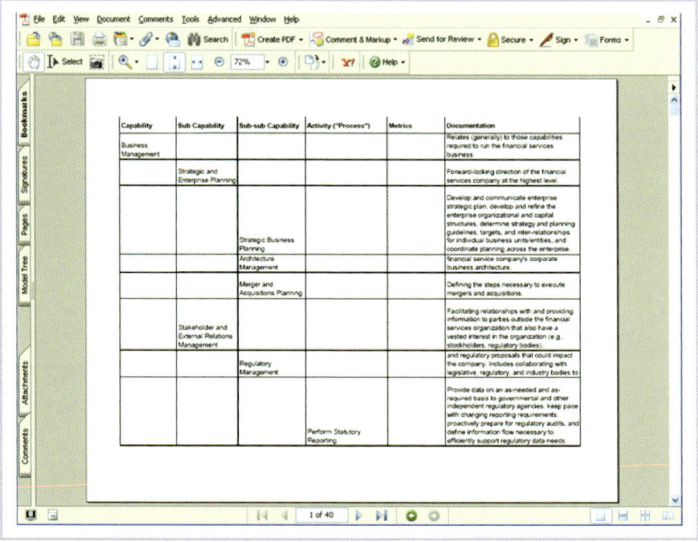

FIGURE 2-3B: Adobe PDF representation of model.

Metamodel Information

Before we go into more detail about the specifics of the model in later chapters, I will describe a few of the stereotypes and icons that are used. These stereotypes and icons extend the base UML model meanings of shapes with ACORD-specific meanings. I've also shown some of the most common core-UML icons for your reference. The following is a listing of the icons used in the model and what each icon represents.

Icon	Name	Description
	Capabilities	an ACORD-specific icon and stereotype used to describe any ability in the insurance industry.
	Class Diagrams	a MagicDraw UML icon and general UML stereotype used for overview diagrams of capabilities and process map elements.
	Relations	a MagicDraw UML icon and general UML concept that indicates that one element is related to another.
	Association	a MagicDraw UML icon and general UML concept that are used to connect relationships between 2 elements.
	Business Process	a MagicDraw UML icon and general UML stereotype that is a collection of activities designed to produce a specific output for a particular customer or market.
	Business Process Diagram	a MagicDraw UML icon and general UML stereotype used for overview diagrams of activities.
	Activity	an ACORD-specific icon and stereotype used to describe a unique process under a capability.

Areas of the Model

This section describes the areas of the model using the MagicDraw modeling tool as the context. The same areas exist regardless of the UML modeling tool, but some of the navigation and visuals may be different for your particular tool.

Capabilities are defined as a baseline of things that insurance companies need to do. These are the business functions that define the industry. The top level capabilities are broken down (in a functional decomposition) further into second and third level capabilities to further define the business abilities (see figure 2-4).

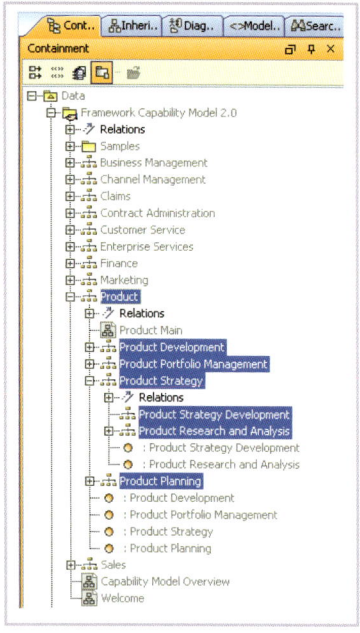 

FIGURE 2-4:
Model capabilities and sub-capabilities.

FIGURE 2-5:
Class diagrams in the model outline.

Within each level of the navigator you will also find other items that are useful. Class diagrams (see figure 2-5) describe the structure of each particular level.

Each class diagram shows you all child elements and the relationships between them. For example, figure 2-6 shows the class diagram for the Marketing capability.

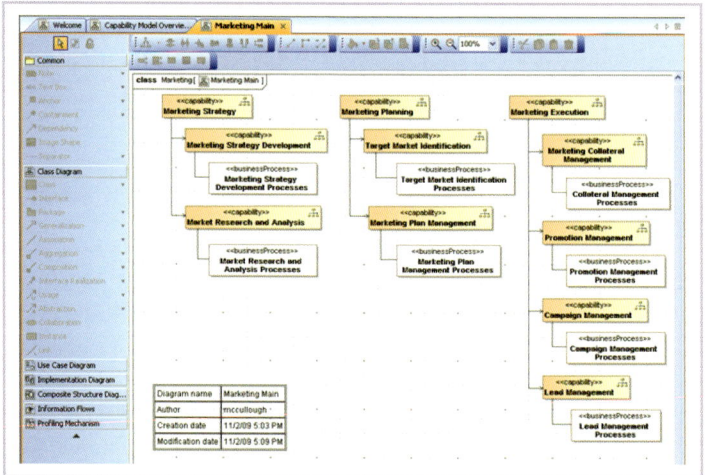

FIGURE 2-6: Marketing capability class diagram.

Associations show how each part of the model relates to any other part of the model contained at that particular level (see figure 2-7). This particular view is not particularly exciting, but it's important to understand the underlying structure of the model.

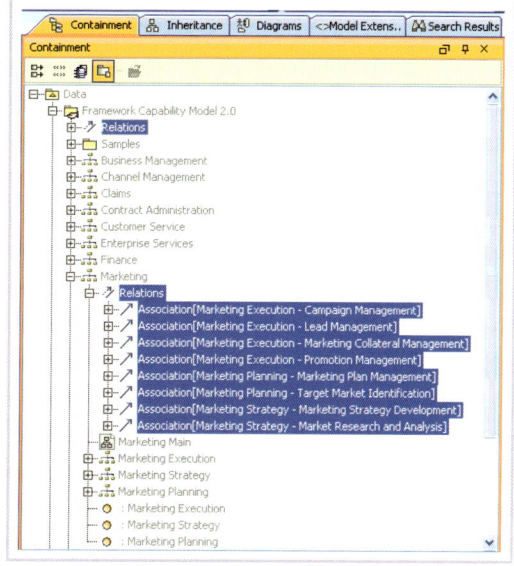

FIGURE 2-7: Relations and Associations.

By clicking on any association you will see the properties for that particular relationship (see figure 2-8). Association properties are also available by double clicking on the relation in the class diagram described earlier.

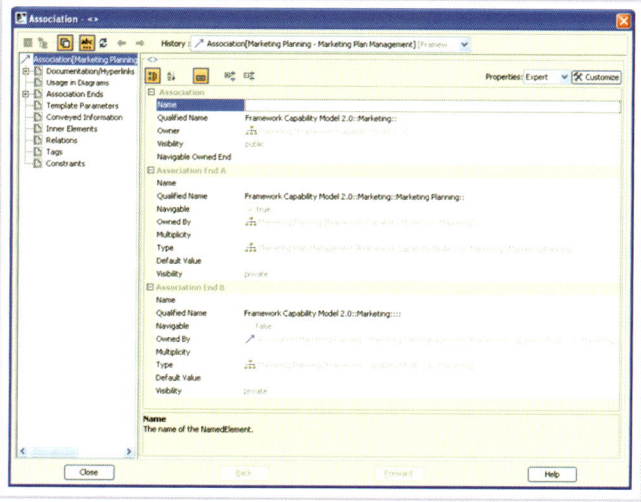

FIGURE 2-8: Association properties.

Third level capabilities may have one or more associated activities, otherwise known as Process Maps (see figure 2-9).

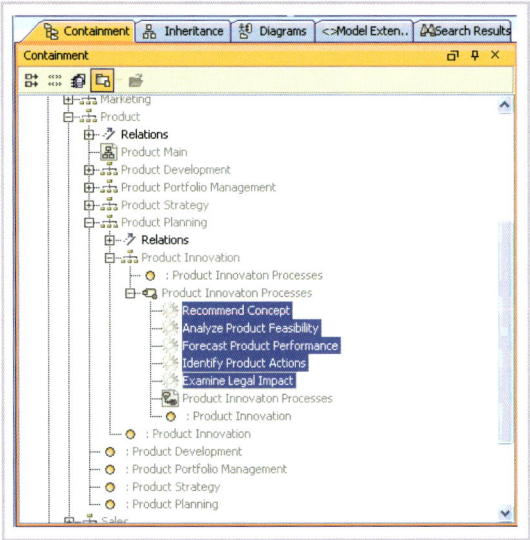

FIGURE 2-9: Activity/Process Maps.

Activity(s) are tasks that can be executed within the capability. You can see these ideas represented in a business process diagram for all tasks under a certain capability by either double-clicking on that capability or digging down to the specific diagram which is associated with a hierarchical one-to-one association on a page (see figure 2-10). The business process diagram just contains the activities, no connections or workflows. However, from here, you can easily create true process diagrams.

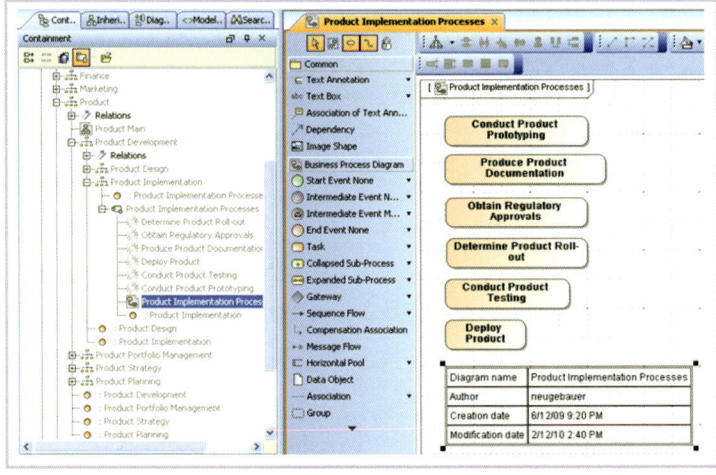

FIGURE 2-10: Business Process Diagram.

Each item in the model contains documentation that gives a definition and (in some cases) an explanation of a particular area. The documentation is viewed by selecting the desired area and clicking the documentation tab (see figure 2-11), scrolling over the desired area (see figure 2-12), or by right-clicking the area and selecting "Specification" (see figures 2-13a and 2-13b).

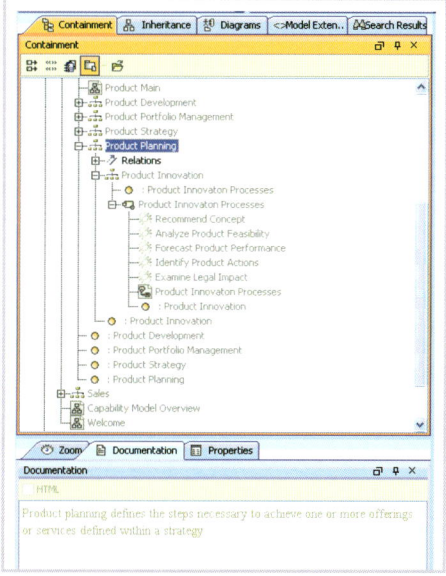

FIGURE 2-11: MagicDraw Documentation Tab.

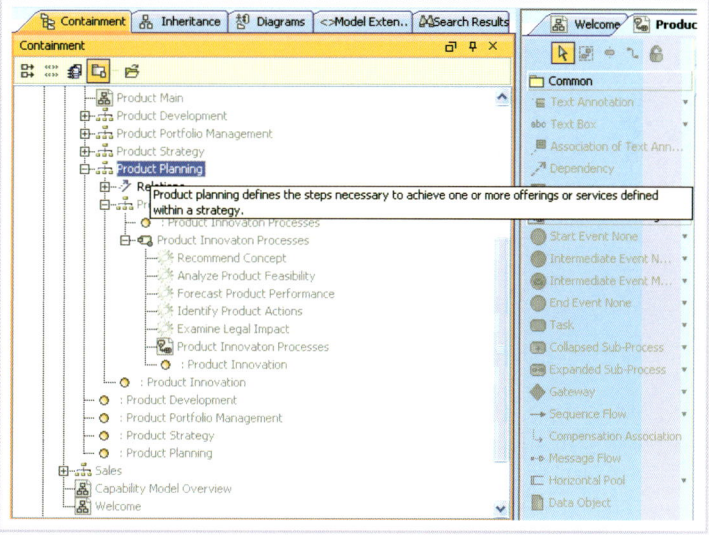

FIGURE 2-12: MagicDraw Scroll over Documentation.

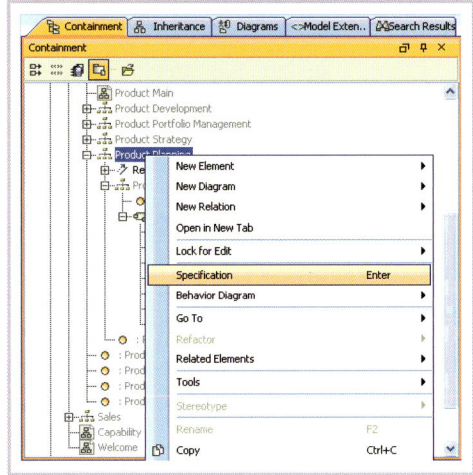

FIGURE 2-13A: MagicDraw Specification Option.

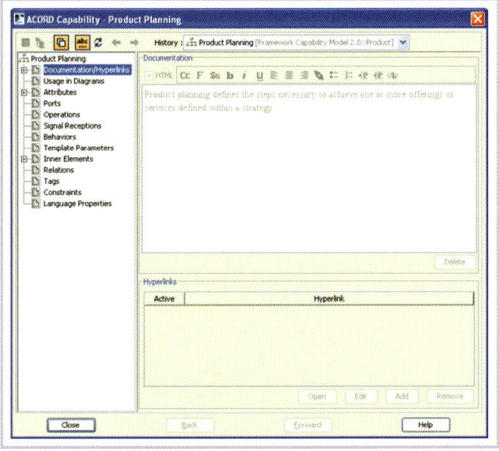

FIGURE 2-13B: MagicDraw Documentation from the Specification.

Summary Conclusion

The items that I covered detail how the model is technically represented, along with information you will need to understand the ACORD Capability Model. The model is available in multiple formats such as HTML, Adobe PDF, Microsoft Excel spreadsheet, UML/XMI, and MagicDraw .mdzip for easy use by the industry. ACORD used the No Magic's MagicDraw modeling tool version 16.5 to create and modify the model and screenshots shown in this chapter. Now you have the concepts and tools you need to start working with the model. Next up is an overview of the model.

The Capability Model: What Insurance Companies Do

The ACORD Capability Model is a model of the functions performed in the insurance business. As Nick explained in chapter two, the functions are decomposed to the level of granularity that represents a step or activity in a business process. The set of functions are collectively referred to as capabilities and the activities are referred to as process maps.

The Capability Model corresponds to the functional components of a traditional business architecture that consists of process, function, and information. As such, it models what is done in the insurance business, not how it is done (i.e., workflow). The Capability Model does not represent a process flow or sequence of activities. The activities contained in the ACORD Capability Model can be steps in a process or workflow, but those processes are not defined in the Capability Model. As such, any capability in the model can be used in multiple processes and workflows.

The Capability Model is comprehensive in the breadth of its representation of the functions performed by an insurance company. The granularity of the capabilities at a given level of the model is consistent across the capabilities. There are specialized functions and activities that users need to add to represent their requirements. In other words, the base Capability Model serves as the starting point. Extensions to the model fit within the structure of the base model rather than requiring changes to the overall structure of the model.

The Capability Model does not attempt a complete representation of all of the activities performed in the insurance business. Variations in process provide competitive advantage for insurers and are far too extensive to represent in a shared model. The Capability Model presents activities at a level that is common across companies and lines of business. Many of the activities can be decomposed into more granular activities depending on how the activity is implemented at a particular company. Companies will extend the ACORD Capability model for the needs of their organization.

The Capability Model is independent of product and line of business. Therefore, the model does not attempt to assign the capabilities to a particular product or line of business. Users of the model may choose to do this in the context of their particular products.

History of the Capability Model

Version 1.0 of the ACORD Capability Model was released in January of 2007. That version was based on a contribution from IBM; the process definitions from their Insurance Application Architecture (IAA). From there, an ACORD working group was formed to validate and modify the contribution and in doing so, the functional and process map delineation was created. That version was released as a Microsoft Windows Help File and is still available today to ACORD members at http://www.acord.org/resources/framework.

In May of 2008, Deloitte, LLC contributed additional content that significantly extended the model, particularly in the Enterprise Support capability. ACORD formed another working group to assimilate the new content and review the first version of the model, taking into account member feedback on version 1.0. While the group was working with the model, it became clear that inconsistencies existed, which were addressed.

Version 2.0 is the product of that working group, which was published in November, 2009. This version is a significant extension and reorganization of Version 1.0. The content of the initial version is in the new version, but in many cases it is positioned differently in the model. Version 2.0 introduces more top level capabilities and structures the capabilities at a consistent level of granularity below the top level capability. As a result, a number of processes are now third level functional capabilities. The processes (activities) are represented by a single level of activities in nearly all cases.

Organization of the Model

The Capability Model consists of ten top level capabilities (Figure 3-1). Each capability uses the <<Capability>> UML stereotype.

Each top level capability is decomposed into two lower level functional capabilities (Figure 3-2).

The third level of capability may contain one or more process activities (indicated by <<businessProcess>> UML stereotype in the model). Not all capabilities in the model have related process activities.

The Capability Model: What Insurance Companies Do

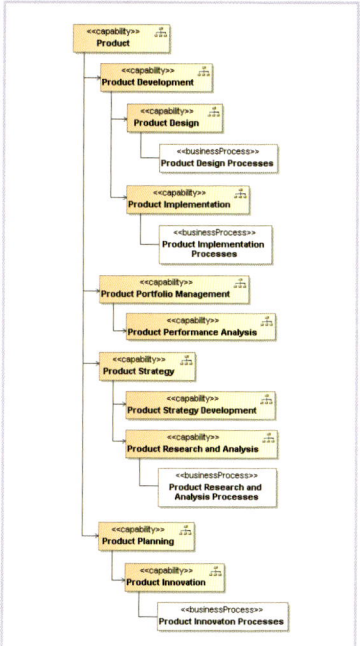

FIGURE 3-1:
Top level capabilities.

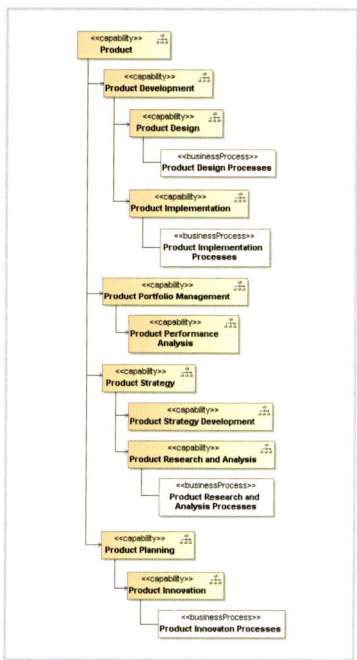

FIGURE 3-2:
Capability hierarchy.

In addition, Deloitte contributed a small number of metrics in Version 2.0 of the model. These metrics are entirely new and while the current content is not significant, the potential for metrics is very significant and the belief is that future releases of the model will contain far more metrics. These metrics are attached to processes in the model.

Nick France provided details on the technical aspects of the model in chapter two.

Getting the Model

The ACORD Capability Model has a very flexible licensing model. There is a $100,000 yearly license fee for non-members to access and use the entire ACORD Framework, but the license fee is, as of the publication date of this book, waived for ACORD members. Please see 'License Agreement for ACORD Framework' (available from ACORD) for further details.

3–17

As an extension to what Nick described in chapter two, and licensing aside, getting the models for ACORD members is very easy.

1. Register at **http://www.acord.org/register**. If you're already registered, skip this step.

2. Log into **http://www.acord.org** with your credentials (new users will have their credentials e-mailed by ACORD Member Services).

3. Select the "Framework" tab on acord.org (see figure 3-3).

4. Scroll down to the model you want (e.g., the Capability Model) and select the "download" link.

5. You will be prompted to accept the ACORD Framework License Agreement– please read this agreement carefully because it represents the limitations to using the models.

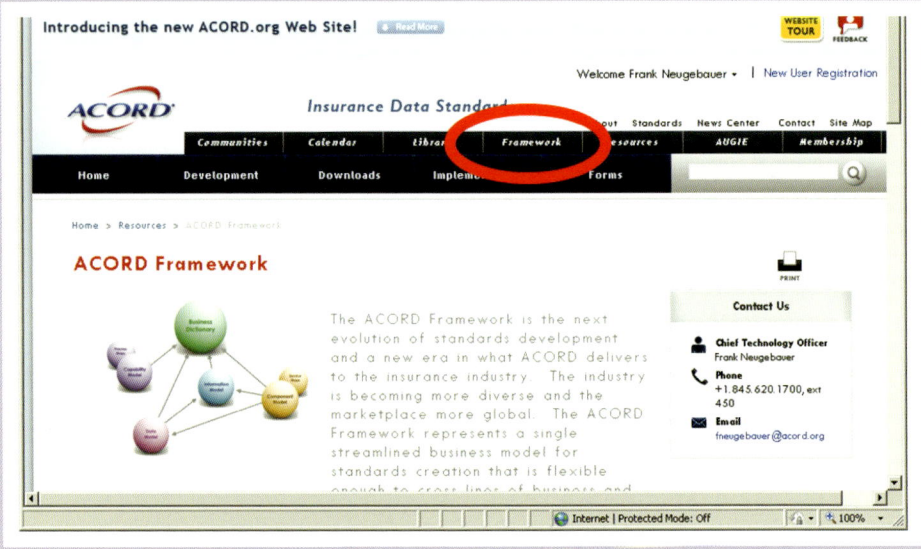

FIGURE 3-3: The Framework tab on acord.org.

In chapter two, Nick France also explained how the model can be unpackaged and used. Now that the basics are completed, it's time to dig into some of the details of the ACORD Capability Model.

What's New in Version 2.0

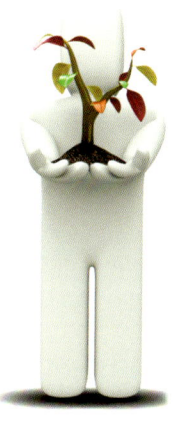

New Content in Version 2 of the ACORD Capability Model

The purpose of this section is to describe the new content delivered in the latest release of the ACORD Capability Model. There are two primary sources of new content in this release: the first is a donation by Deloitte, LLP ("Deloitte"), which resulted in the call for a working group to incorporate the donation into the model. The second source is the contribution of the many ACORD members who participated in the weekly working group sessions to refine and enhance the model, bringing their individual experiences and perspectives to benefit the industry.

The donation was set in motion by a review of the ACORD Capability Model Version 1 in late 2007. Deloitte recently refreshed versions of its own Life and Annuities and Property and Casualty capability models. After completion of their models, they decided to conduct a quick assessment against the ACORD model to see how it compared. Deloitte realized that a gap existed between the models; the Deloitte models had more content.

Deloitte then initiated a more formal analysis to document the gaps, and shared those findings in a working session with ACORD. Deloitte's primary ACORD contact at that time, suggested this would be a great addition to the ACORD Capability Model and collectively, ACORD and Deloitte agreed on the terms of the donation based on ACORD's Intellectual Property policy. Announced at the ACORD/LOMA Insurance Systems Forum in May, 2008, the contribution from Deloitte consisted of 49 capabilities and 123 processes.

In addition, Deloitte decided it might be interesting to the membership to discuss metrics in the context of the Capability Model. They selected seven metrics from Deloitte's Global

Benchmarking Center and its ACES[1] and LIONS[2] expense studies to include as part of the donation. Aligning these metrics to capabilities or processes enable a discussion amongst ACORD members on the potential value of building a complete set of metrics to support the model.

The Capability Model Working Group began incorporating the donation into Version 2 in the fall of 2008. A number of ACORD members from both the carrier and vendor communities participated in the weekly sessions to build out the model. This work included not only incorporating the donation, but restructuring the model and bringing entirely new ideas to the table to improve it. Once the basic model had been completed, the team worked to add and refine all the definitions that give the model its context. The work was completed in the fall of 2009, and the new model was released and presented at the ACORD Implementation Forum shortly thereafter.

As always, the quality and usability of the ACORD deliverables are a testament to the commitment of its members, and everyone involved appreciates the time and effort expended by the working group members over that twelve month period.

Structural Changes

Version 1.0 of the Capability Model contains five top level capabilities. Each capability is broken down into two lower levels of functionality. With the exception of the Enterprise Support capability, the lowest level of capability is decomposed into one or two levels categorized as processes. All capabilities in the model are numbered using a format of 1.2.3.4.5 with each position corresponding to a level in the hierarchy. The capabilities and processes are presented in separate Windows Help files.

The granularity of the top level capabilities varies significantly. Customer Service includes Policy/Contract, Claims Management, and Relationship Management, while Marketing and Product Management contain only those areas. This results in inconsistent model content across all levels of the hierarchy. The primary structural change in Version 2.0 increases the number of top level capabilities from five to ten. Consistency in the level of detail across the levels of the hierarchy across the entire model was a key goal of the working group.

This re-leveling results in much less depth in the processes. In nearly all cases there is one level of processes within the third level capability. In addition, the Enterprise Support capability in Version 1.0 has been split into Enterprise Services, Business Management, and Finance, with processes for most of these capabilities.

---

1. ACES–Annuity Contract Expense Study, a benchmarking of line-of-business and information technology operations specifically for annuity providers.
2. LIONS–The Life Insurance Operations Study, a benchmarking of line-of-business and information technology operations specifically for life insurance providers.

The basic pattern for capabilities consists of capabilities around strategy, planning, management, and execution. This basic pattern has been extended and modified in accordance with common business practices. In a number of cases the model uses the term "management" to include both management and execution capabilities when that is standard practice in the industry

Version 2.0 of the model is based on a business view of capabilities. It does not group capabilities by abstract functional categories (analysis, management, planning, strategy, design, etc.). Analysis capabilities are not grouped under a parent Analysis capability but are instead located within the business capability that depends on the analysis. Version 2.0 of the model does not attempt to provide views of the model other than the business view, but the model can be extended by the user to have views by functional categories. Similarly, the model does not reflect an information technology view. There is no Business Intelligence capability, nor is there a Reporting capability. These are treated as types of software applications, not business capabilities. IT capabilities are in the model under Enterprise Services and are independent of any business capabilities that might be automated by information technology.

Version 1.0 of the model is semantically inconsistent. The IAA contribution was based on a defined, controlled vocabulary. Much of Version 1.0 of the Capability Model was rewritten without using the IAA vocabulary. The IAA semantics remained largely in process names and in some definitions. Version 2.0 of the model is written using terms agreed to by the working group as representative of common industry usage. It is not built on a controlled vocabulary, neither IAA nor one defined by the working group. It has not been reconciled semantically with the ACORD Business Dictionary (yet).

Given the semantic inconsistency in Version 1.0, much of the capability documentation is imprecise, sometimes seeming to be in conflict with the capability name. In version 2.0 all of the documentation has been reviewed and revised for clarity and consistency with the capability name.

The intent of the Capability Model is to document capabilities, not to imply an execution flow across those capabilities. The numbering of processes in Version 1.0 tends to imply a sequence of execution of the processes. In some cases the processes are repeated within different capabilities in order to document the steps in a workflow. Version 2.0 eliminates the numbering and strives to keep the Capability Model totally independent of any sequence of execution. Many capabilities may be executed in a sequential manner as part of a workflow, but the Capability Model should not be interpreted as specifying a sequence of execution based on the positioning of any of the capabilities of the model relative to each other.

Version 1.0 includes a Capability to Line of Business (LOB) matrix that relates capabilities to product groups. Version 2.0 drops this matrix because the capabilities are defined independent of any particular product. Organizations using the Capability Model can map the capabilities to the lines of business they support.

Top Level Capabilities: An Overview

The premise for the ACORD Capability Model is that any industry's business architecture is based on a set of discrete business functions referred to as capabilities. These capabilities define WHAT the business does, and can be broken down functionally. How these capabilities are performed (workflow and business rules) usually determine a company's level of differentiation and competitive advantage. The ACORD Capability Model serves as the foundational layer of the required business capabilities that the insurance industry does or could do across the insurance industry value chain.

An example is Contract Lifecycle Management, which consists of the various skills required to handle financial service agreements. This capability falls within Contract Administration—the capability to create and manage financial services agreements.

The capability model provides the "inventory" of insurance industry capabilities. Some capabilities are unique to a domain or can be shared across domains (Property & Casualty/Surety, Life & Annuity or Reinsurance/Large Commercial). An example of a shared capability is "Underwriting." Still other capabilities are used across the entire enterprise and are packaged into the Enterprise Services top-level capability.

How can the model be used by the Industry and ACORD Membership?

In chapter seven Dave Schmitz explains uses of the model in detail, but in short, the model can be used to:

- Communicate the nature of the business in business terms.

- Assist with organizing or re-organizing the structure of the business.

- Identify the common and unique industry capabilities and areas for ACORD standards asset reuse.

- Provide the basis for the definition of business process models and business process service definitions.

- Identify merger and acquisition opportunities.

- Jumpstart an application portfolio strategy.

- Assist with project portfolio management.

- Help your organization understand its capability maturity versus the industry as a whole.

- Identify where existing ACORD Standards can be leveraged and where opportunities exist for further development of ACORD standards.

Additionally, the Model sets the foundation for the insurance industry to define their business architecture. For these purposes, Business Architecture is the outline/blueprint of the business. This type of architecture provides a reference framework that enables the alignment of the business needs with the current and planned IT solutions. This ensures that the IT solution(s):

- Meet the business needs (function and ROI).

- Respond to business changes.

- Are more cost effective.

This chapter covers the top-level capabilities to provide a comprehensive overview of the model as a whole, highlighting the breadth of the model. In chapter six, Dave Jones digs into the Product capability, showing you the depth of the model.

The Ten Capabilities

At the top of the functional decomposition are ten core capabilities that collectively represent the fundamental nature of insurance across lines of business and geographies.

Top Level Capabilities: An Overview

Notice that the capabilities are in general terms and can easily represent the business units of a financial services company. That's why the model is ideally suited to help you understand your organizational structure.

While most of the capabilities are self-contained (e.g., Claims), several of the capabilities are used throughout the organization. For example, Enterprise Services is specifically for capabilities used by the other capabilities; information technology is a good example. Furthermore, Business Management is a general capability that exists to run the business and runs throughout the other capabilities implicitly.

Business Management

Running a financial services company requires general management skills at the highest level of the organization for things such as strategic planning, stakeholder relationship, and enterprise effectiveness. The Business Management capability is broken down into just those kinds of sub-capabilities.

You will find planning capabilities (e.g., Merger and Acquisitions Planning), regulatory management, investor relations, and process management within the model (among many others). Collectively, these core capabilities "run the business."

On the activity, or process map, level, you will find (for example):

- Perform Statutory Reporting

- Perform Claims Regulatory Compliance

- Identify/Implement Process Improvements

5–25

These process maps are randomly chosen from the model but give you the basic level of detail for the processes within the Business Management capability and sub-capabilities.

Channel Management

The distributions channels of insurance are of critical importance in insurance because for many companies, it represents the main source of income. The Channel Management capability is about establishing and maintaining distribution channels and supporting organizations. For example, captive, independent agent, and direct (e.g., Internet) channels are all included.

There are five sub-capabilities of Channel Management that includes channel development, channel strategy, producer management, channel execution (e.g., managing producer agreements), and channel planning. Those five sub-capabilities decompose further with additional capabilities.

The extensive process maps are categorized as:

- Producer Agreement Development Processes
- Producer Support Development Processes
- Producer Recruitment Processes
- Producer Effectiveness Management Processes
- Producer Agreement Administration Processes
- Producer Compensation Processes
- Producer Support Processes
- Producer Production Planning Processes

Those process map categories exist throughout the model (e.g., Producer Support Processes is connected to the Producer Support capability) and provide an illustrative way to understand the kinds of processes the model support.

Claims

[<< capability >> **Claims**]

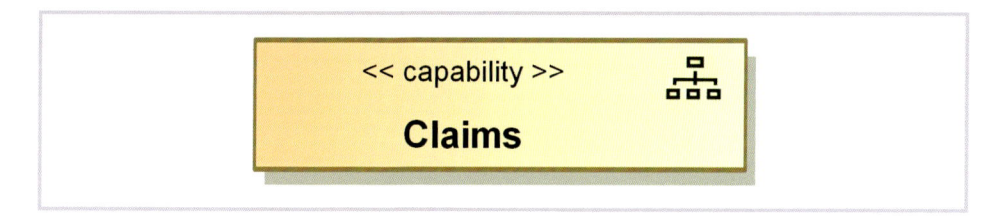

It's very easy to understand that a financial services company must be capable of handling claims. What may not be obvious is how significantly the claims capability breaks down after that high level capability. This capability includes everything from claims lifecycle management (including notification, fraud management, recoveries, and dispute resolution) to claims strategy and planning. For obvious reasons, this capability is critical for insurance companies to understand because a proper claims capability can save money and increase customer satisfaction.

Second-tier capabilities include Claims Lifecycle Management, Fraud Management, Claims Handling, Claims Recovery, Dispute Resolution, and Claims Inquiry. Then of course there are the third level capabilities, which are hinted at by the process maps described next.

The ACORD Capability Model has many process maps for claims, which are categorized by their parent capabilities, including (but not limited to):

- Claims Notification Processes (e.g., Validate Claim)

- Fraud Management Processes (e.g., Detect Potential Fraud)

- Claims Handling Processes (e.g., Determine Claim Settlement)

- Claims Recovery Processes (e.g., Recover Subrogation)

- Dispute Resolution Processes (e.g., Manage Litigation)

- Claims Analytics and Reporting Processes (e.g., Produce Claim Reports and Statistics)

- Catastrophe Planning Processes (e.g., Simulate Loss Projections)

In all, there are over 40 capabilities and process maps within Claims.

Contract Administration

<< capability >>
Contract Administration

Undoubtedly the most important capability in the model is Contract Administration not only because it represents the fundamental element in insurance, but also because it involves the primary revenue generator for a financial services company. Generally speaking, Contract Administration involves capabilities and process maps for creating and modifying insurance contracts.

Sub-capabilities include Contract Investment Administration and Contract Lifecycle Management (within which are more capabilities). You will also find process maps for things like disbursements, underwriting, contract issuance, and contract change management.

One element of this capability worthy of an extension is for non-policy contracts. The ACORD Information Model (another facet of the ACORD Framework) defines intermediary contracts, which are for agreements between a financial services company and its providers (for example).

Customer Service

<< capability >>
Customer Service

The documentation for the Customer Service capability states that this capability is meant to, "Manage the relationship of the financial services organization with existing (and potential) customers and stakeholders of the organization's products." The top-level sub-capabilities are Customer Relationship Management, Customer Relationship Strategy, and Relationship Planning. All of that information shows that the Customer Service capability is customer relationship management (CRM) in a fairly pure sense. Sub sub-capabilities include (but are not limited to):

- Customer Interaction Management

- Customer Analytics

- Customer Retention Strategy

- Service Bundling/Customization

Some of the process maps within the aforementioned capabilities include:

- Manage Customer Inquiries

- Manage Customer Requests

- Administer Customer Information

- Analyze Customer Buying

- Define Interaction Methods

Enterprise Services

<< capability >>
Enterprise Services

The basic idea for the Enterprise Services capability is for abilities that are shared throughout an insurance company. As such, this is a significantly larger capability than most. With over 93 capabilities and process maps, it is (in fact) the largest part of the model. Deloitte's contribution had the largest impact on this capability, especially in the area of human resources.

The second-level capabilities in this model (which break down into a significant number of sub-sub capabilities) include:

- Facilities Management

- Information Technology Management

- Procurement

- Human Resources Management

- Project Management

- Risk Management

The process maps for Enterprise Services, which also gives you a glimpse at the types of sub-sub capabilities, include:

- Manage Partner Contracts
- Manage Strategy
- Headcount Planning
- Manage Skills Assessments
- Design Organizational Structure
- Manage Employee Satisfaction
- Source (Job) Candidates
- Manage Benefit Inquiries
- Manage (Employee) Performance Metrics
- Manage Pay Slips
- Maintain Project Iteration Plans
- Maintain Project Templates
- Audit Line of Business Operations
- Manage Reinsurance Requirements
- Determine Loss Control Services
- Determine Risk Appetite

A good area to focus on in order to understand the nature of Enterprise Services is the Human Resources (HR) capability. It's clear that HR is needed for the entire organization, and is not standalone in that regard. In other words, Enterprise Services are used by the organization at large.

Finance

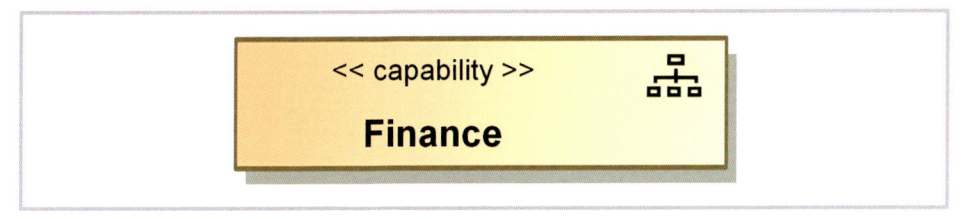

In many industries there is often ambiguity around the difference between finance and investments, which is especially true in insurance. The ACORD Capability Model defines the Finance area strictly to planning for and managing the capital assets of the company. To remove the ambiguity, Finance includes investments, which is intuitive since investments are logically a sub-part (or sub-capability as the case may be) of Finance.

The sub-capabilities give you a better idea of the meaning and content of the capability as a whole:

- **Financial Management**–including Investment Management, Tax Management, and Financial Reporting (among others)

- **Financial Planning**–including Investment Planning, Budgeting, and Capital Project Planning (among others)

- **Billing and Payments**–including Billing and Collection and Payment Management

- **General Accounting**–including Accounts Payable, General Ledger, and Fixed Asset Management (among others)

The process maps within the Finance capability include (but are not limited to):

- Monitor Investments

- Analyze Reserves

- Implement Investment Execution

- Create Capital Budget

- Administer Invoicing

- Issue Payment

Collectively, you can see that the capability involves the financial assets of the company and how those assets are planned for and managed.

Marketing

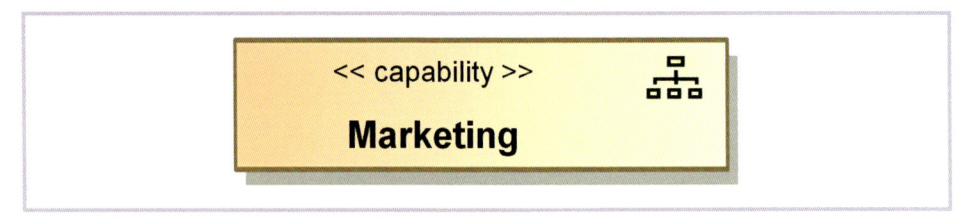

> << capability >>
> **Marketing**

Insurance companies must help current and potential customers understand their brand and the products they offer. The Marketing capability provides capabilities and process maps to do just that. The sub-capabilities are:

- **Marketing Strategy**–develop the goals, objectives, and approach to achieving those goals and objectives

- **Marketing Planning**–the actions necessary to execute the strategy

- **Marketing Execution**–making the marketing strategy a reality

Within those sub-capabilities are a number of sub sub-capabilities including:

- Marketing Collateral Management

- Campaign Management

- Market Research and Analysis

- Target Market Identification

Finally, some of the process maps randomly selected from the aforementioned list of sub sub-capabilities include:

- Develop Market Messaging

- Execute Marketing Campaign

- Perform Pricing Analysis

- Perform Market Segmentation

The Marketing capability is not meant to create the idea of marketing in the general sense, but rather to focus marketing as it relates to insurance. This goal is accomplished by limiting the content of the capability and process maps to only the core of what's required.

Product

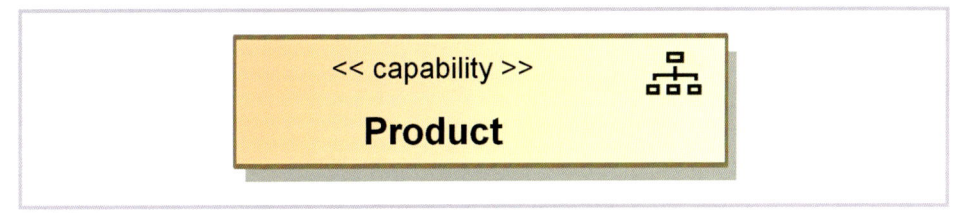

> **<< capability >>**
> **Product**

The Product capability includes defining and managing the insurance products offered by the financial services company. This critical capability includes the following sub-capabilities:

- **Product Development**–including Product Design and Product Implementation

- **Product Portfolio Management**–including Product Performance Analysis

- **Product Strategy**–including Product Strategy Development and Product Research and Analysis

- **Product Planning**–including Product Innovation

Process maps within this capability are categories by their sub sub-capability including:

- Product Design Processes (e.g., Define Product)

- Product Implementation Processes (e.g., Obtain Regulatory Approvals)

- Product Research and Analysis Processes (e.g., Conduct Product Market Analysis)

- Product Innovation Processes (e.g., Forecast Product Performance)

Note that this capability is explained in total within chapter six by Dave Jones.

Sales

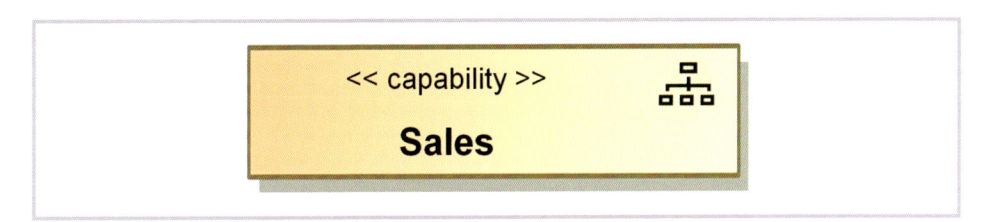

> **<< capability >>**
> **Sales**

Selling the products or services of the financial services organization is distinct from defining or marketing those products and services, which is why Sales is its own capability. As of version 2.0, the capability is slight, but you may have extensive capabilities and processes that can easily be added to the foundation provided by the ACORD Capability Model.

The ACORD Working Group that created version 2.0 took existing elements from version 1.0 and isolated them within the Sales capability. The intent is for this capability to grow in subsequent versions of the model.

Contract Acquisition is the sole (yet critical) sub-capability of the model and is concerned with selling policies or services. The Sales Execution capability is the sole sub sub-capability of Contract Acquisition and it includes the following process maps:

- Perform Needs Analysis

- Provide Quote

- Apply for Insurance

- Initiate Insurance Application from Quote

Now that you have gotten a top-level summary of the entire model, David Jones from Nationwide Insurance is going to explain the Product capability in totality.

Detailed Overview–Product

Product Overview

A product is something an insurance company offers or provides to its potential and existing customers. Products are assembled into a package that is sold to customers. Most products define agreements that the insurance company could enter into with a customer, but products may include services provided by the insurance company. Service products are usually provided as part of a product that is sold as an insurance contract between the insurance company and the customer.

Products are distinct from, and managed separately from, contracts. The Capability Model has separate capabilities for Product, Contract Administration, and Contract Acquisition (in the Sales capability). A contract is based on a specific product. A product is related to many contracts in various states (quotes, active contracts, terminated contracts, etc.). A contract is always related to a specific version of a product.

Insurance contracts are composed largely of coverage products packaged into a policy product, which is the product offered to consumers. Groups of products which define a policy contract may be grouped into larger "products" that include package policies. They may be grouped further into lines of business, so that an insurer may have an "auto" product that is composed of a number of products offered to customers (e.g., standard, non-standard, and residual product offerings).

Products are complex constructs; they include rules that constrain the allowed variation in contracts based on the product, including underwriting rules, premium calculation rules, product composition rules (you can purchase coverage A or coverage B, but not both), and conditions for when coverage is provided. Products have rules that define the actions, called requests, that can be performed on a product (quote, issue) and on a contract created from the product (cancel, reinstate, endorse). Products contain rules that specify what attributes (information) are needed to create a contract from the product, as well as rules that constrain product attributes values (available coverage limits, e.g.). Products specify the relationship of people, objects, money and other things to the product as roles in the product. Products also specify the investment strategy for premium investment, options for investing premiums, rules for pricing and reserving the product, distributing the product, and many other things as defined in the Product Design processes in the Capability Model.

Functional Decomposition–Product

Product capabilities cover all aspects of defining and managing the insurance offerings and services available from the financial services company. They include defining the insurance company's product strategy, planning product actions, managing the product portfolio, and developing products (including product changes and product implementation), as shown in figure 6-1. Product capabilities do not include any capabilities related to contracts based on the product. These capabilities are in the Marketing, Sales, and Contact Administration capabilities in the model.

FIGURE 6-1: Product Capabilities.

Product Strategy

The Product Strategy capability includes capabilities that define the corporate direction for offerings and services. These capabilities may include defining the importance of product to the company (e.g., first mover or follow-on). Product Strategy includes researching products in the marketplace as well as internally and defining how the company will compete with product offerings (see figure 6-2).

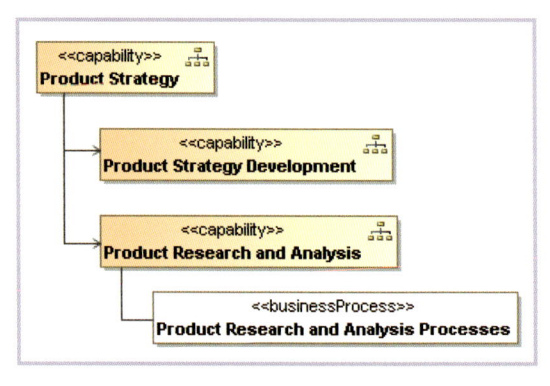

FIGURE 6-2: Product Strategy.

Product Strategy Development

Product strategy development sets the company direction for insurance offerings and services. It must be based on a thorough understanding of industry product trends and opportunities and internal product, contract, and claims management capabilities. Within this sub-capability, it's easily conceivable that users can add processes for developing such strategies including marketing and regulatory considerations.

Product Research and Analysis

Product Research and Analysis gathers information on product opportunities within the industry. It includes information gathering about how products from various companies are accepted by consumers and how existing similar products are performing in the marketplace. Performance of products offered by the company (current and past) may be included in the analysis. The information gathered and developed within the Product Research and Analysis capability forms the basis for developing the company's product strategy.

Product Planning

During Product Planning, the steps necessary to execute on a product strategy are defined. These steps include identifying opportunities related to introducing new products, modifying existing products, and withdrawing products. Product planning may be driven by both internal and external events and conditions, including regulatory and legal actions. The Product Planning capability does not include the definition of specific new products or product modifications; it extends only to identifying what actions to take to carry out the product strategy.

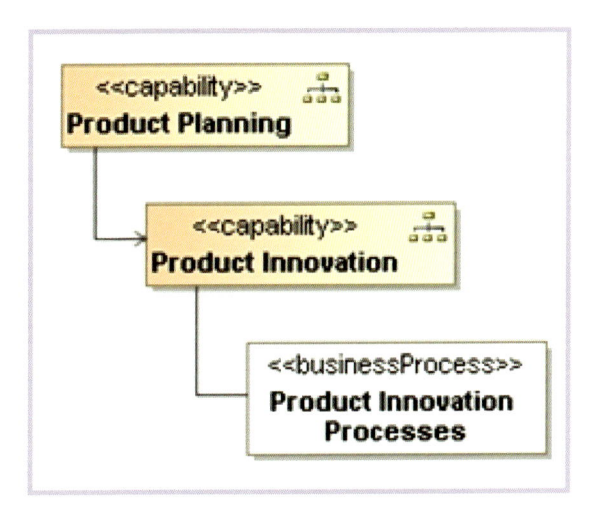

FIGURE 6-3: Product Planning.

Product Innovation

Product Innovation includes defining what new products should be developed and what changes should be made to existing products to make them more competitive, profitable, or in alignment with regulatory constraints. This capability includes creating product concepts and ideas, evaluating their feasibility, predicting their performance, understanding their relationship to legal constraints, and identifying actions to take once these factors are understood.

Product Portfolio Management

Product Portfolio Management coordinates all of the products a company has or has had, along with potential new products. Portfolio Management assures that the company's entire portfolio aligns with and contributes to effectively carrying out the product strategy. Portfolio management takes in product strategy, product plans, and information about the performance of current product offerings and evaluates that information to identify actions that need to be taken to the service portfolio.

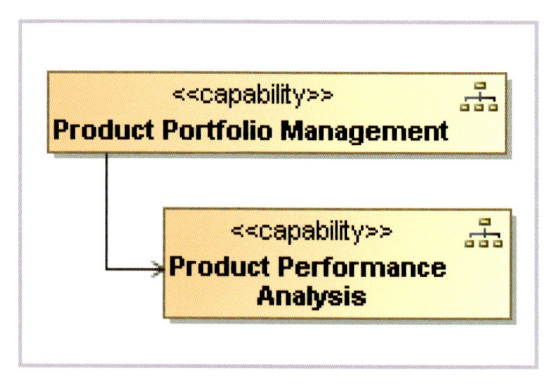

FIGURE 6-4: Product Portfolio Management.

Product Performance Analysis

Product Performance Analysis monitors the performance of products using metrics such as market penetration, profitability, and risk and analyzes the resulting data to provide relevant information for managing the product portfolio.

Product Development

Product development supports the design, enhancement, and implementation of new and existing products. It executes the high-level product plans that result from product portfolio management and product planning, resulting in the ability to create contracts and provide services based on a fully defined product with all product management and support capabilities in place and functioning.

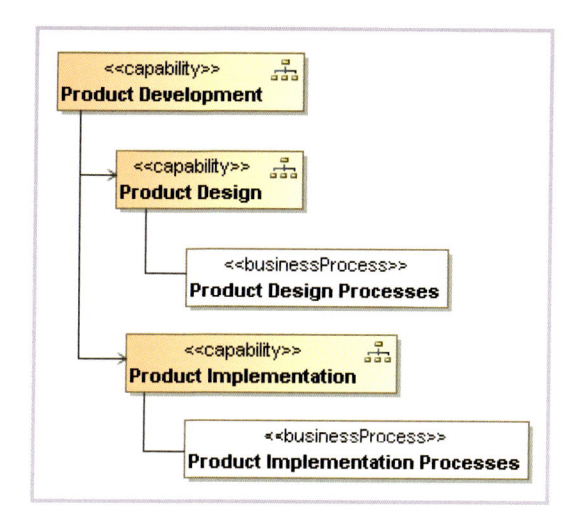

FIGURE 6-5: Product Development.

Product Design

Product design defines all aspects of a new product or of changes to an existing product. The Product Design Processes in the model define the various activities that are performed as part of product design. Product design must be completed prior to Product Implementation.

Product Implementation

Product Implementation includes capabilities for introducing a new product or product changes to the marketplace, including regulatory approval, product documentation, roll-out schedule definition, product testing, prototyping product performance through simulations, and training.

Product Process Maps

Product process maps document the activities a company undertakes to implement capabilities within processes. As previously noted, the capability model does not provide workflow for how these activities are related within processes, nor does it provide a detailed model of how these activities are performed. The manner in which the activities are performed will vary by company. How a company performs these activities determines how effective the company is in a capability and can provide competitive advantage for the company. The Capability Model does not attempt to specify how activities are performed. It only identifies activities normally performed by a company as part of a capability.

The Capability Model does not attempt to be exhaustive in identifying activities within capabilities. A company utilizing the Capability Model should extend the model with activities specific to their business. Product activities may vary by the type of product being acted upon.

Product Research and Analysis

Product Research and Analysis process maps include activities that are performed in support of all product capabilities. They are located in one place in the model, under the Product Strategy capability, because the research and analysis will not normally be conducted separately for each second level capability in the model. The Product Strategy capability, as the highest level driver of product direction and actions, was chosen to hold the research and analysis process maps.

Conduct Product Market Analysis

FIGURE 6-6: Product Research and Analysis Processes.

Conduct Product Market Analysis

Conduct Product Market Analysis gathers information about how products are performing in the marketplace and analyzes that information to provide insights for developing a company's product strategy, managing the product portfolio, planning product actions, and developing and implementing products. The product information may include information on other company's product in addition to products of the insurance company gathering or analyzing the information.

Product Innovation

Product Innovation activities take product ideas from concepts and prepare them for consideration relative to a company's product strategy and product portfolio management. If a product idea is approved as a result of this consideration it will be taken up by the Product Development processes and turned into an available product.

FIGURE 6-7: Product Innovation Processes.

Recommend Concept

The Recommend Concept activity develops product ideas and brings them to a place they can be evaluated at a conceptual level. This involves developing ideas for many of the product characteristics that are fully defined in the Product Development capability, but without the rigor present in that capability.

Analyze Product Feasibility

Analyze Product Feasibility considers whether a product concept is viable in the marketplace, is consistent with the company's product strategy, and whether it can be implemented, given the company's capabilities in all the areas that are necessary to implement and support the product concept.

Forecast Product Performance

Forecast Product Performance is the process of predicting how a proposed product will sell in the marketplace and the degree to which it might contribute to profitability.

Identify Product Actions

Identify Product Actions is the process of determining what steps must be taken to bring a potential product into the marketplace. This process prepares a product concept for design and implementation.

Examine Legal Impact

Examine Legal Impact is the process of determining the legal implications of introducing a potential product into the marketplace, including whether legal and regulatory concerns preclude introducing the product and whether there are legal constraints that need to be addressed in defining the product.

Product Design

Product Design processes take a product concept that has been approved for implementation and defines the details of the product, how it will be managed, distributed, underwritten, rated, reserved, marketed, and reinsured. Once a product has been designed it is ready to be implemented into the marketplace.

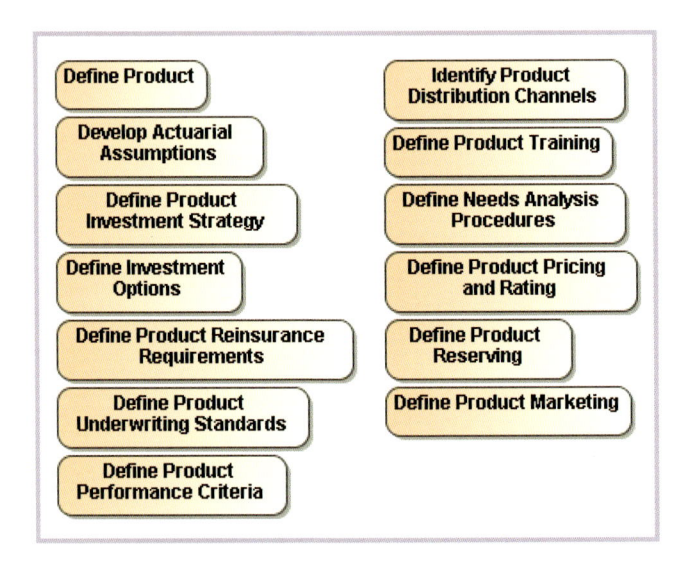

FIGURE 6-8: Product Design Processes.

Define Product

The Define Product activity takes a product concept that has been approved for implementation and defines all of the details of the product, including product composition, bundling, product rules, calculation rules, requests, roles, and attributes.

Develop Actuarial Assumptions

Develop Actuarial Assumptions defines the basis for pricing the product. It does not include the detailed development or premium calculation formulas.

Define Product Investment Strategy

The Define Product Investment Strategy process determines the approach that will be taken for managing any investment components that are part of a financial services product.

Define Investment Options

Define Investment Options determines the investment choices to be offered for a financial services product that contains investment components.

Define Product Reinsurance Requirements

The Define Product Reinsurance Requirements process identifies the reinsurance needed to assist in managing product risk.

Define Product Underwriting Standards

Define Product Underwriting Standards is the process of identifying the rules for accepting a specific risk under a product.

Define Product Performance Criteria

The Define Product Performance Criteria process identifies the financial results required to make a product viable in the market place. Metrics can play an important role in developing such criteria.

Identify Product Distribution Channels

Identify Product Distribution Channels is the process of determining which distribution channels sell and service a product. Distribution channels include both internal and external distributors.

Define Product Training

Define Product Training determines the education required for selling, servicing, and managing a product. This includes building awareness of a product within the organization and its distribution channels, but does not include marketing the product to existing and potential customers.

Define Needs Analysis Procedures

The Define Needs Analysis Procedures process identifies the criteria used to determine if a customer or prospective customer will benefit from a product. This may include a workflow with specific steps and guidelines for working with prospects, but does not include defining detailed underwriting rules for the product.

Define Product Pricing and Rating

Define Product Pricing and Rating applies the actuarial assumptions defined for a product and determines the detailed calculation rules for pricing the product and calculating premium for contracts based on the product.

Define Product Reserving

The Define Product Reserving process determines the approach and detailed rules for setting aside (reserving) monies to cover losses incurred against a product.

Define Product Marketing

Define Product Marketing determines how a product will be promoted, including brand identity, advertising, marketing collateral, and campaigns. The creating of marketing campaigns and collateral and the building of a brand identity is not part of the product capability, but part of the marketing capability. The Define Product Marketing capability determines the approach to marketing for a specific product, not the execution of that approach.

Product Implementation

Product Implementation processes take a fully designed product, verify that it is ready to implement, obtain regulatory approvals, create the necessary documentation and support structures, determine the product roll-out, and deploy the product for distribution.

- Conduct Product Prototyping
- Produce Product Documentation
- Obtain Regulatory Approvals
- Determine Product Roll-out
- Conduct Product Testing
- Deploy Product

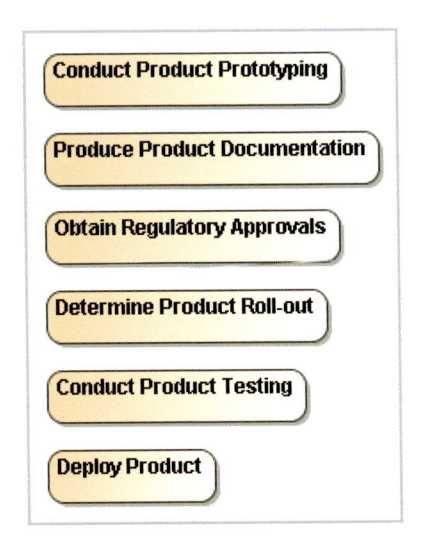

FIGURE 6-9: Product Implementation Processes.

Conduct Product Prototyping

Product prototyping is done to simulate a product's performance in the marketplace prior to making the investment in deploying the product. This effort may build on earlier efforts to predict the performance of the product by using a fully detailed product definition and more sophisticated simulation tools and techniques.

Produce Product Documentation

Produce Product Documentation is the process of creating materials that describe a product. The product documentation may be produced for internal use, external use with regulators and distributors, and external use with prospects and customers. The product documentation may be used by other processes that create marketing materials, training materials, and other communications about the product.

Obtain Regulatory Approvals

The Obtain Regulatory Approvals process includes all aspects of acquiring permission from governing bodies to sell a new or modified product.

Determine Product Roll-out

Determining the roll-out of a product determines the sequence for introducing a new or modified product into the marketplace.

Conduct Product Testing

Product testing introduces a product into a controlled test market for the purposes of determining the feasibility of rolling the product out to a wider market. This process does not include the testing of information technology assets developed to support the product, which is part of the Information Technology capability.

Deploy Product

Deploy Product is the process of introducing a product into a market. This process serves primarily to coordinate the execution of multiple related capabilities; these capabilities may precede the start of selling the product (information technology deployment, marketing collateral creation, advertising promotion and marketing campaign planning) and may continue or commence once the product is deployed (e.g., claims handling).

Capability Model Uses–An Overview

There are a broad range of strategic and tactical uses for the ACORD Capability Model within an insurance company. Recently I have seen similar models discussed primarily in the context of Enterprise Architecture or Business Architecture, and in fact a capability model can be one of the foundational components of a holistic architecture methodology. While these are excellent uses for such a model, I believe the core value of the ACORD Capability Model resides in improving communication and providing an organizational framework.

The Capability Model as a Communication Tool

As a communication tool, the Capability Model offers an easy, visual way to represent a consistent view of what an insurance company does. It provides a standard point of reference and a common lexicon to the diverse set of constituents of an insurance company, thereby improving understanding and enabling alignment of business priorities and objectives across the organization. While the end result in the form of the Capability Model is useful, the process of collaborating across the organization–from all functional divisions to IT and corporate functions-on the customization of the ACORD Capability Model is in itself a highly effective way to build understanding and acceptance of the concept and use of such a model.

For example, a typical challenge in most companies is the alignment of business and technology personnel. Frequently there are miscommunications caused by each speaking in their own language, resulting in a lack of clear comprehension by the other party. Business resources may not fully grasp the operational impacts of IT goals, and similarly technology resources may not understand the business objectives and how IT can support them. In this case, aligning stakeholders to a Capability Model and leveraging a common lexicon increases the level of understanding.

Similarly, often times a clear link between proposed technology changes and business value derived from those changes is not effectively communicated. In such cases, a business case mapped to the Capability Model serves as an effective tool for technologists to understand the desired impact business stakeholders are looking for and assists the business team in understanding the impact the solution will have on business operations. In both of these examples the Capability Model provides the common language to help increase both the efficiency and understanding between business and technology personnel.

The Capability Model as an Organizational Tool

Another challenge faced within the insurance industry is the absence of a framework that allows firms to organize business functions in a standardized way. As part of the overall ACORD Framework, the Capability Model provides a consistent structure to organize business and systems artifacts. Using it as an organizing framework across artifacts in an insurance company can enable stakeholders to quickly understand how things fit into the operation. As people become more familiar with the model, they will quickly assess what impacts them, and focus their time and attention on things that matter most with regards to their responsibilities.

For example, frequently a new structure is created to organize project artifacts, or even project leadership structure, for any new business or technology project. Using the Capability Model can reduce the time and effort involved with developing this structure, and it also provides a familiar model team members will recognize. Or, when no organizing framework was used in the past, the structure provided by the model can increase productivity for both those creating project artifacts and those consuming them. An added benefit of the Capability Model is that it can help to facilitate the completeness of most work efforts.

Another example of the organizational construct exists in how technology assets are viewed by business people. Often it can be difficult to explain how a portfolio of hundreds of technology applications is supporting business operations. Aligning applications with capabilities provides a map for business people to better understand how applications support the business. Additionally, the Capability Model provides visibility to redundant applications and capability gaps.

The Capability Model Decomposition

The ACORD Capability Model is developed at an enterprise level, consisting of both core operational business functions (e.g. new business, claims) as well as corporate functions (e.g., technology, accounting) that you will find in any insurer. Figure 7-1 provides a macro view of the model representing the top level capabilities. A model developed at this level has many uses, but as you review the various different options for using the model you will find that you may need to decompose and expand the model to support specific needs. For example, the baseline model should easily support high level analysis such as project portfolio management; however, more focused efforts, such as evaluating software requirements in a specific function, require additional detail.

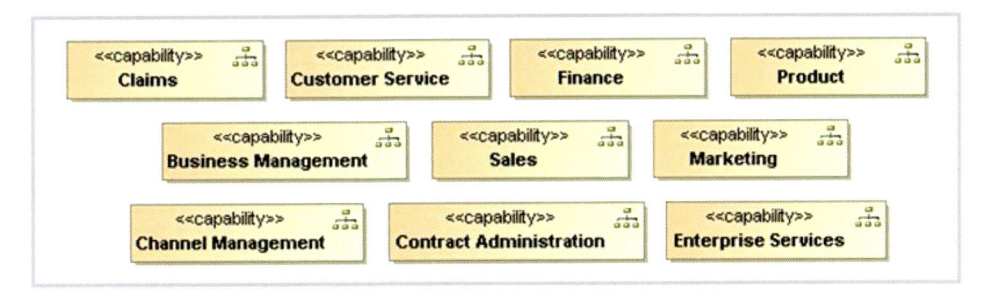

FIGURE 7-1: Macro View of ACORD Capability Model.

There are two options for activities requiring more granularity than the three levels of capabilities provided by the current model. One option is to use the process level of the capability. However, the use of processes instead of capabilities may not support the activity being performed. If that is the case, a second option is to leverage the process level to derive a more detailed set of capabilities. Each organization will need to determine the appropriate level of granularity and their preference for process versus capability for each use of the model. This method will become clearer as you see examples later in this chapter.

The remaining sections in this chapter describe some of the more common and effective uses of the ACORD Capability Model. As mentioned previously, while it can serve as a foundational component of a holistic architecture methodology, leveraging the Capability Model to define business and technology architecture is a complex topic requiring substantial organizational commitment. For the purposes of the following sections in this book I discuss discrete uses of the model to solve specific and typical challenges insurers face. This is not an exhaustive list, but it provides enough information to understand how using the Capability Model broadly within an organization can help improve communications, efficiency, and understanding.

Capability Model Uses– Business Aligned IT Strategy

Frequently IT strategies lack support from the business community. Sometimes this is a function of the relationship between business and IT, while other times it is a product of miscommunication or the inability of business and IT to get to a common understanding of what the business requires. Regardless, IT strategies that are misaligned to current and future business needs are likely to result in inefficient deployment of capital and disappointed business stakeholders.

While IT strategies should exist in the context of value to the business, some aspects of the IT strategy are driven by technology considerations. For example, replacing unsupported software or improving disaster recovery are both providing value to the business by limiting risk. Similarly, the implementation of an improved integration environment provides value to the business through increased agility and lower costs to support future systems integration efforts. Additionally, investments made to improve technology delivery, such as skills development, IT process improvement, and infrastructure changes generally provide substantial benefit to the business.

Still, a good IT strategy is founded on technology improvements that are aligned to and support the business strategy, and the Capability Model can be a key enabler. Comparing a business strategy and a business operating model (the operating environment for the business strategy–shows how people, process and technology enable the business strategy) to the Capability Model highlights business capability changes required to support the strategy. Additionally, the Capability Model aligned to a business strategy helps to identify technology investments needed to achieve strategic objectives.

Example

There are many different ways that the Capability Model can be used in support of IT strategy development. A common method is to use the Capability Model to identify target areas in need of change to support the business strategy. For the purposes of this example, assume the business strategy calls for targeting specific products to more granular market segments than had been used in the past.

Step one is to identify capabilities impacted by this strategy by reviewing each capability and determining the potential to either support or be impacted by the strategy. Looking at the Product capability presented earlier in this book, you might review the Product Performance Analysis capability and identify it as a candidate to support this strategy. There are obviously many other capabilities that are impacted, and the assessment must occur across the Capability Model to facilitate full coverage. Note that this assessment can be driven by strategy (assess all capabilities in the context of a given strategy) or driven by capability (assess all strategies in the context of a given capability or capability group) with equal effectiveness.

Capability Model Uses—An Overview

PRODUCT

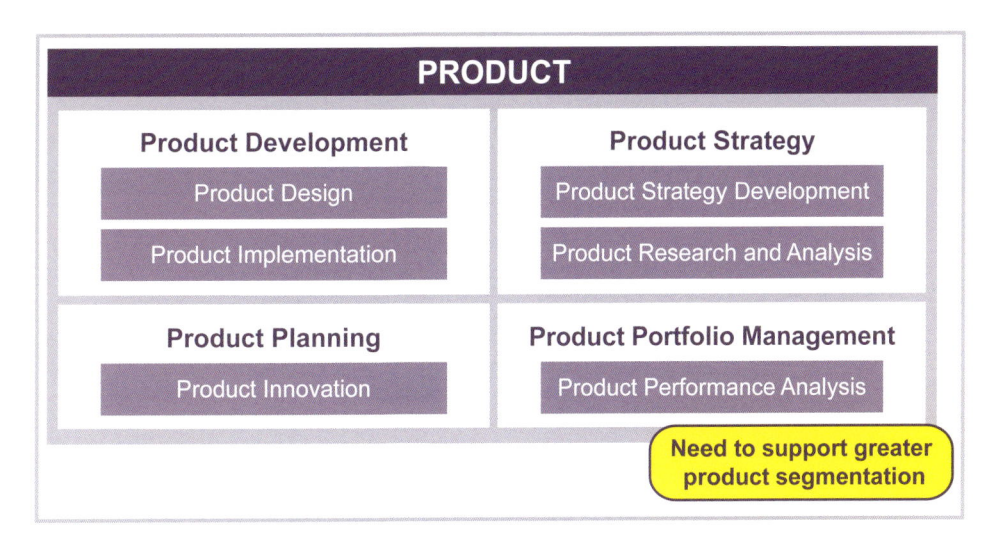

Product Development	Product Strategy
Product Design	Product Strategy Development
Product Implementation	Product Research and Analysis
Product Planning	**Product Portfolio Management**
Product Innovation	Product Performance Analysis

Need to support greater product segmentation

FIGURE 7-2: Business Strategy Mapped to Product Capability.

Step two is to identify the specific opportunities or needs within each impacted capability. Ideally this process occurs collaboratively with business and IT leadership. In addition to providing a more complete analysis, engaging both the business and IT prepares leadership across the organization to support the eventual IT strategy. In this specific example, it may be determined that market penetration analysis needs to occur at a more granular level of segmentation to measure performance of the new strategy. Opportunities within other capabilities should also be captured (e.g., capture of data, provisioning of data).

Once all opportunities have been identified, aligned to the business strategies they support, and consolidated within the Capability Model, the model provides a full view of capabilities required to support the business strategy. IT can now evaluate the required capabilities to identify the projects it would need to perform in order to support them. Since applications generally align to the capabilities they support, the model simplifies the process for the technology team and enables identification of potential synergies across the portfolio.

As noted previously, there are also other IT initiatives that directly and indirectly impact business operations and influence the effectiveness and efficiency of the IT organization. These investments must also be aligned to the business capabilities and strategies they support. This consolidated list of IT projects and initiatives should be rationalized against each other, and provided with at least a rough-order-of-magnitude sizing/cost. You will now have a comprehensive list of IT initiatives that are clearly linked to the business capabilities and business strategies they support.

Since the demand for technology services generally far exceeds the available IT capacity (dollars, resources, and capabilities), standard governance and prioritization processes now take over. With the linkage of how each technology initiative supports the business strategy providing a common foundation, the stage is set for developing an IT strategy that is in alignment with and understood by both business and technology leadership.

Capability Model Uses–Organizational Alignment

Frequently insurance organizations are aligned by function within a broader line-of-business or business unit hierarchy. Using the Capability Model can support assessment of your organization's functional alignment and allow you to more clearly identify potential gaps and conflicts in accountability, execution, and scale. The Capability Model provides a common structure for the analysis and the ability to easily link it within the broader context of the business architecture.

Examples

Showing leadership accountability in the context of the Capability Model can quickly identify potential issues. In figure 7-3 the leadership resources have been mapped to the areas on the Capability Model that they believe they are accountable for. A simple review indicates that C. Hams seems to have overlapping accountabilities with both J. Sims and B. Boyd. Additionally, there is no one in the organization who believes they are accountable for Product Portfolio Management. The Capability Model provides a representation of the capabilities needed to operate your business and can help you align responsibilities and ensure coverage across your operations.

PRODUCT

J. Sims — Product Development	C. Hams	Product Strategy — B. Boyd
Product Design		Product Strategy Development
Product Implementation		Product Research and Analysis
J. Sims — Product Planning		Product Portfolio Management
Product Innovation		Product Performance Analysis

FIGURE 7-3: Leadership Accountability Mapping.

Adding the functions that are supported by resources associated with each leader can provide another view into potential challenges. In figure 7-4 each of the leaders has been color coded, and the capabilities that are supported by each of their respective teams are circled with that same color. This view provides additional visibility to the overlapping leadership accountability between the Product Development and Product Strategy domains. Additionally, while an accountability gap was previously identified in the Product Portfolio Management space, looking at the team mapping shows that there are resources supporting this function from two different teams.

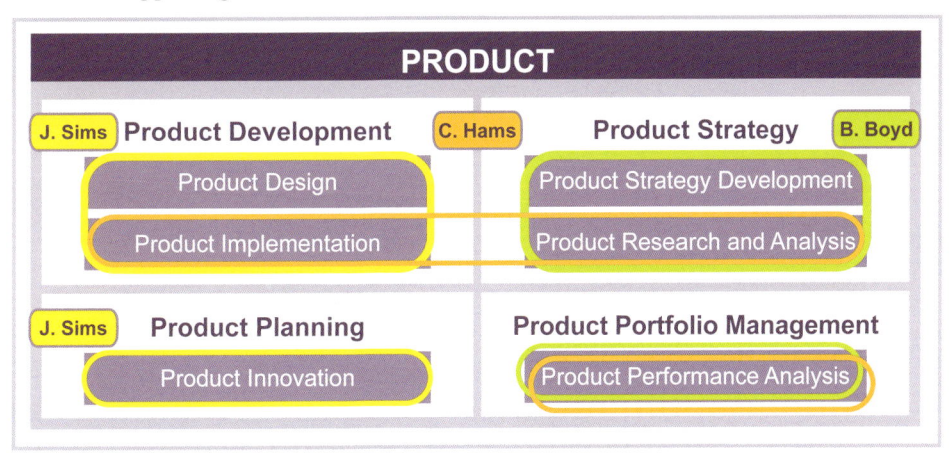

FIGURE 7-4: Team Mapping.

Other opportunities to use the Capability Model for organizational assessment include identifying the number of Full Time Equivalent resources (FTE's) associated with each function, understanding what capabilities a specific organizational unit is supporting, and identifying resources who support a role regardless of placement within an organization. As a final example, reviewing FTE's in the context of the Capability Map can identify outliers in terms of the number of resources supporting different functions. Figure 7-5 provides an FTE view for the Product capability, and in this case the leadership team might be surprised by the number of FTE's supporting Product Portfolio Management–an observation that might indicate potential issues with the availability, quality and access to data.

FIGURE 7-5: FTE Mapping.

Capability Model Uses–
Application Portfolio Strategy/Management

Application Portfolio Strategy (APS) and Application Portfolio Management (APM) can both benefit from use of a Capability Model. Before discussing how, it is important to distinguish the difference between APS and APM. APS is the point in time development of a systems application strategy to align to your future state business and technology needs. APM is the ongoing management of systems and applications to optimize a technology portfolio from application implementation to retirement. In both cases, leveraging a Capability Model highlights how the application portfolio supports the business and provides a an effective tool to execute APS and APM initiatives.

Example

When developing an application portfolio strategy (APS), the objective is to understand how the current portfolio of applications supports both current and future state business functionality and technology architecture needs. The Capability Model can be an effective tool to support the former.

Maturity models can be created that expand on the Capability Model with more specific capability descriptions. These capability descriptions are set across a maturity matrix. In a simple model, you might categorize capabilities as baseline or as leading/innovative (see figure 7-6) to help business leaders identify the target state capability level. In more complicated models there is a continuum of capabilities across 4 to 5 categories from "early stage" through "industry leading" where business leaders can plot both their current state along with the desired target state (not pictured).

Capability	Capability Description		Desired Target Size
	Baseline	Leading/Innovative	
Product	• Minimal prototype/test marketing efforts	• Established target customers and sample tests group	• TBD
	• Reactive product offerings based on competitive pressures	• Established product goals for existing clients to support client retention	
	• Etc.	• Etc.	

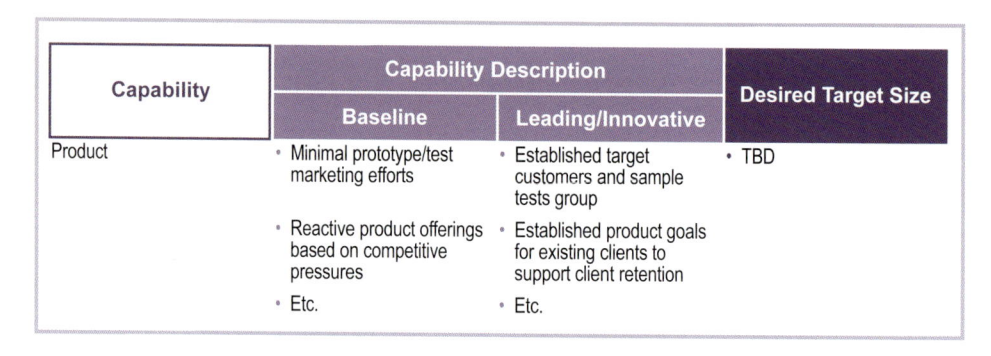

FIGURE 7-6: Sample Capability Assessment Framework from Deloitte.

Understanding the desired target state is only the first step in an APS exercise. The next step is to assess how well your current applications support the desired target state. Figure 7-7 adds a column to the assessment framework to identify the system supporting that business capability and whether it currently supports each target state capability or, if it does not, how significant the effort is to close the gap.

Capability	Capability Description		Desired Target Size	Current Systems Support
	Baseline	Leading/Innovative		
Product	• Minimal prototype/test marketing efforts	• Established target customers and sample tests group	• TBD	• System name- supports today or high/medium/low gap
	• Reactive product offerings based on competitive pressures	• Established product goals for existing clients to support client retention	• TBD	
	• Etc.	• Etc.		

FIGURE 7-7: Application Assessment Against Target State Business Capabilities.

A simple method to summarize the extent of the gaps in the application portfolio is to color code the Capability Model, where those capabilities whose desired target states are effectively supported by current systems are green, those where the gaps are moderate in frequency and scale are yellow, and those where the gaps are more severe in orange (figure 7-8). This allows stakeholders to easily view where the strengths and weaknesses of the current applications are from a business perspective.

PRODUCT

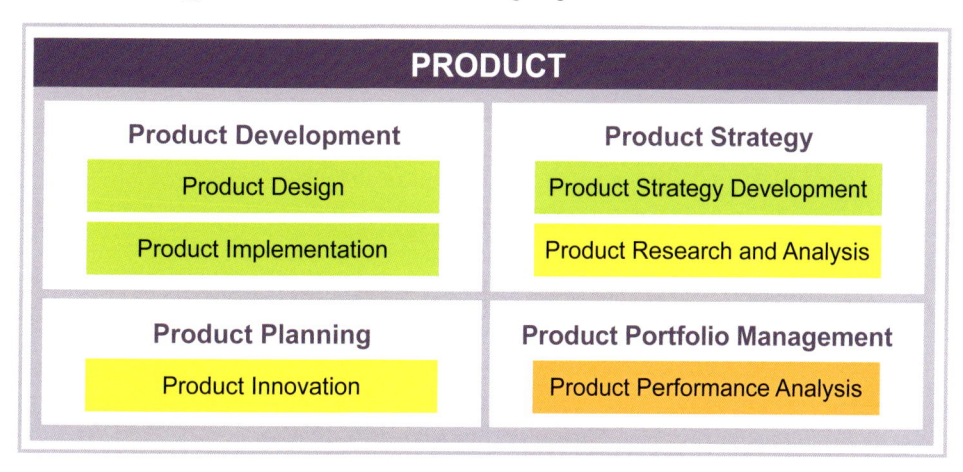

Product Development	Product Strategy
Product Design	Product Strategy Development
Product Implementation	Product Research and Analysis

Product Planning	Product Portfolio Management
Product Innovation	Product Performance Analysis

FIGURE 7-8: Sample Capability Model–Systems Support View.

In order to support the sequencing of the application portfolio strategy, there needs to be a business prioritization. The target state capabilities can be prioritized within the hierarchy and context provided by the Capability Model. This process tends to be fairly simple within a top level capability (e.g., Product), but becomes much more difficult when capabilities impact multiple areas of an organization. Still, through coaching and the use of some additional workshop tools, business and technology leadership can be quickly facilitated through an appropriate prioritization exercise.

Recognize that the model only provides the business input into the APS, and the technology team must also evaluate the current applications against their target state architecture (or reference architecture) and other technology requirements. Technology leaders must also prioritize the gaps and issues with those current applications. It is the marrying of the prioritized gaps between business and technology assessments that forms the foundation for the final APS. Initial hypothesis and sequencing need to be established, and then adjusted to accommodate dependencies, capacity, and other constraints.

Moving on to the maintenance of your application portfolio, there are a number of tools in the marketplace that support APM. They provide guidance for managing the portfolio though an application lifecycle (i.e., a classification of life stages of an application). Examples of application life stages might be "maintain", "invest and extend", or "retire." There are many different attributes captured and evaluated as part of an APM program. Alignment to business value and categorization of how they support the business are critical. Using the ACORD Capability Model enables you to understand potential redundancies across the application portfolio and it also provides a context for determining the business value of an application.

If you are using a commercial APM tool, its reporting feature will likely support analysis with the Capability Model categorization. This provides a common framework already understood by the organization to enable easier consumption of the outputs. In the absence of a formal APM tool, you can manually map applications against the Capability Model (figure 7-9)–in this case we have mapped applications and tools as both are used to support certain business functions. This view of the Capability Map allows you to easily identify where you have application support for business capabilities, where you have potential redundancies, and where you have gaps. Depending on your objectives you can color code the capabilities (per maturity model example previously) or the applications and tools to identify APM categorization (not shown).

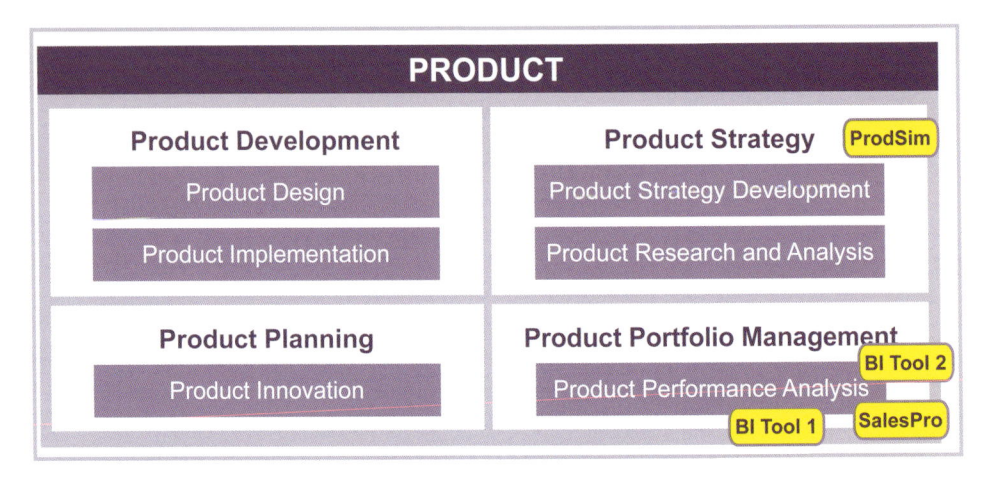

PRODUCT	
Product Development	**Product Strategy** [ProdSim]
Product Design	Product Strategy Development
Product Implementation	Product Research and Analysis
Product Planning	**Product Portfolio Management** [BI Tool 2]
Product Innovation	Product Performance Analysis [BI Tool 1] [SalesPro]

FIGURE 7-9: Application Mapping to Capability Model.

You can enhance figure 7-9 in many different ways to visually express other analyses of the application portfolio. You can color code or otherwise annotate the applications to demonstrate how well they support the business capability, show their technical quality (how well they align with target state architecture), identify their current lifecycle stage, or any number of other valuable insights.

Note that there are many APM artifacts that may not leverage the Capability Model—for example, a graphing of applications by business value versus technical maturity with a cost sizing. However, the Capability Model enables the applications to be easily viewed in a business context, and will support more effective communication with stakeholders.

Capability Model Uses—Systems Development

The Capability Model can be a valuable tool in supporting a broad array of systems development activities. Whether conducting a software vendor evaluation, developing a future state business process model, or developing a new system (regardless of software development lifecycle methodology), the Capability Model provides a way to organize project activities and align project resources with a common taxonomy and language to support development activities.

To support systems development activities, the Capability Model generally needs to be at a greater level of detail than the current ACORD model. Considering a project in the product domain, the current model might need to be extended one to two levels deeper in order to provide sufficient granularity. The reason this level of detail is necessary is the complexity and volume of artifacts generally required in systems development activities. If your model is at too high a level, the benefits of the organization may be lost.

Example

As previously mentioned, the first step is to take the model down one to two levels. This can be accomplished in multiple ways. Reviewing the Product capability (figure 7-10), the Product Development category could have Product Design and Product Implementation both broken out into component capabilities to expand the level of granularity. Another option is to take Product Design and Product Implementation, and identify the component capabilities within each of them as distinct levels in the capability hierarchy. The appropriate level of granularity is more art than science, learned over time from experience, but the main point is that a level of expansion and customization is probably required to attain the required level of granularity.

PRODUCT	
Product Development	**Product Strategy**
Product Design	Product Strategy Development
Product Implementation	Product Research and Analysis
Product Planning	**Product Portfolio Management**
Product Innovation	Product Performance Analysis

FIGURE 7-10: Product Capability.

With the Capability Model at a granular enough level, its taxonomy can be used throughout the development lifecycle. For example, it can be used to drive the overall structure of a project (i.e., the phasing of the work for requirements, design, development, testing, and implementation). Having the Capability Model at the center of the phasing strategy allows the team to remain synchronized, with the common point being the business functions supported as defined by the model.

As another example, when conducting a software vendor evaluation, the Capability Model helps to structure a standard set of requirements for vendor assessment. Using a Capability Model provides a framework for business stakeholders to define requirements, organize requirements for presentation to the vendors, and define priorities for scoring vendor responses.

The steps and visual examples are too complicated to share in this book, but the different ways that a Capability Model can be used in support of systems development activities are almost endless. The key is to recognize that you need the model to be at an appropriate level of detail for the activity at hand.

Capability Model Uses– Project Portfolio Management

The governance processes in place to support project portfolio management (PPM) can be improved by leveraging a Capability Model. In addition to providing a standardized framework for organizing projects, it integrates business context that increases the level of understanding across an organization. The Capability Model can be enhanced by using color coded views to demonstrate strategic priority, business or technology pain points, and capability maturity.

Capability Model Uses—An Overview

Leveraging the Capability Model is only one component of an overall PPM program. Assessment of the portfolio to accommodate IT supply and demand, resource skill sets and availability, return on investment, individual project performance (e.g., over budget, behind schedule), dependencies, and other factors are all part of a successful PPM program. Still, mapping projects to/against capabilities provides an easy way to evaluate how initiatives align with business priorities.

Example

Figure 7-11 displays active projects applied against a Capability Map. Color coding can be used to represent business priority, capability maturity, current pain points of business operations, or a combination. Plotting projects against this color coded model provides visibility to whether the projects are aligned with highest priorities. In this example I have assessed business stakeholder perception of the quality of systems support for these functions, and color coded green where the application is well supported, yellow where support is adequate, and orange where there is the greatest gap.

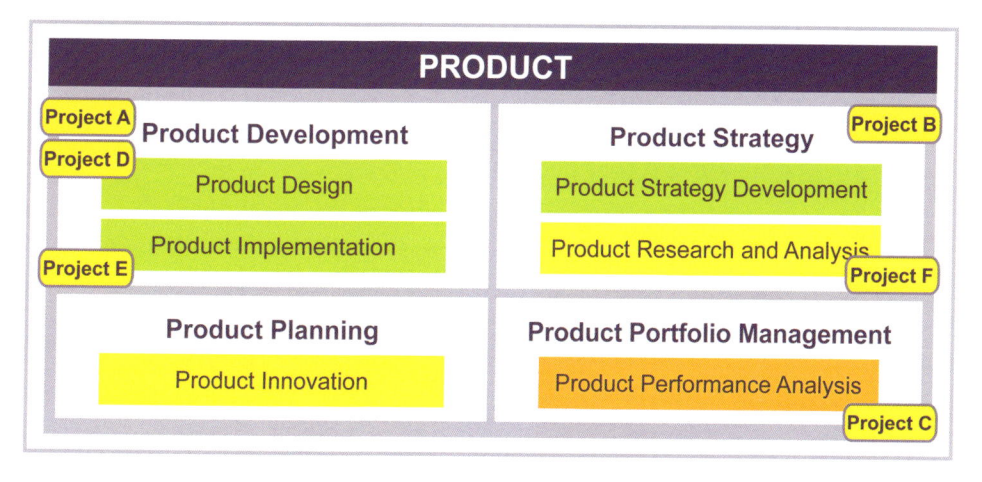

FIGURE 7-11: Projects Mapped to Capability Model.

In this case it appears that Product Performance Analysis (in orange) is in the greatest need, yet the majority of projects are supporting other capabilities in the Product domain. This might necessitate a re-evaluation of the other attributes of the PPM program to confirm that the portfolio is appropriate. You can also enhance the graphic by color coding or adjusting the size of the project bubbles to demonstrate scale (e.g., total spend).

In addition to enabling assessment of project alignment with the greatest needs within the organization, mapping projects to the Capability Model can help technology to understand how projects impact the business, and can provide the business with a clear understanding of the business functions that are impacted by the project portfolio. Again, at its core, the

Capability Model is a tool to help improve communication and alignment and reviewing projects in the context of business capabilities provides an easy way for stakeholders to understand where the project spend is being applied.

Capability Model Uses–Mergers and Acquisitions

A frequent challenge when engaged in the early stages of a merger is to understand the footprint of each organization, particularly regarding people and technology. Using the Capability Model can provide a common structure that helps enable the organization to quickly assess some of the dimensions and complexities of the consolidated operation. It also lays the foundation for the more detailed analysis required to plan and execute merger integration activities.

Example

There are two Capability Model mappings that can be performed to better understand the consolidated resource footprint of an organization. The first is at a leadership level, where you can take the first n levels of each organization (n being the depth to which you wish to go in your first pass, generally 3 levels deep) and map these key leaders to capabilities that are within their area of responsibility. It can be very useful to have the following data associated with each leader–company, name, location. Figure 7-12 provides a pictorial view of what a leadership mapping might look like. After completing an initial view of the organization, you can continue to go deeper in the org chart to get the level of detail desired.

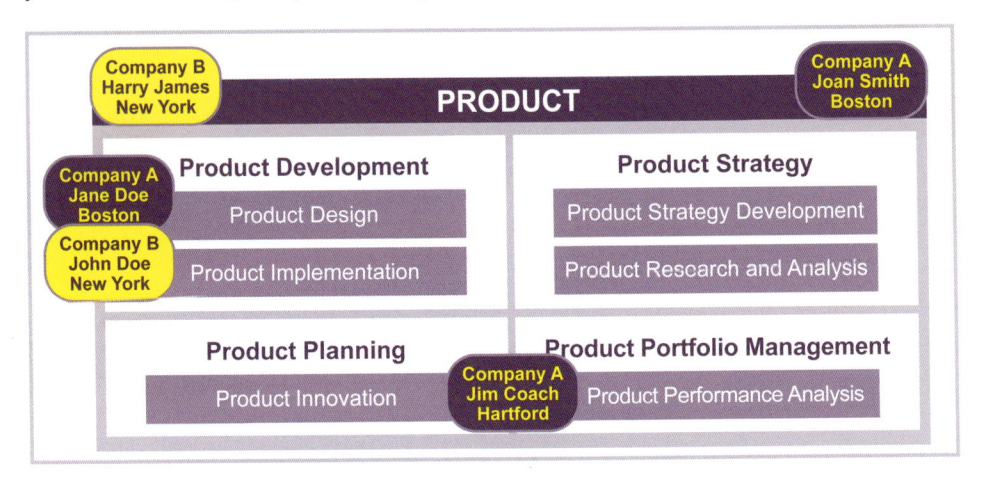

FIGURE 7-12: M&A Leadership Mapping.

Another useful view of the resource footprint is to capture total resources by location in support of each function. Figure 7-13 provides a pictorial view of such a personnel

Capability Model Uses—An Overview

mapping. You have flexibility to place resources at whatever level in the Capability Map that makes sense for the analysis you are performing.

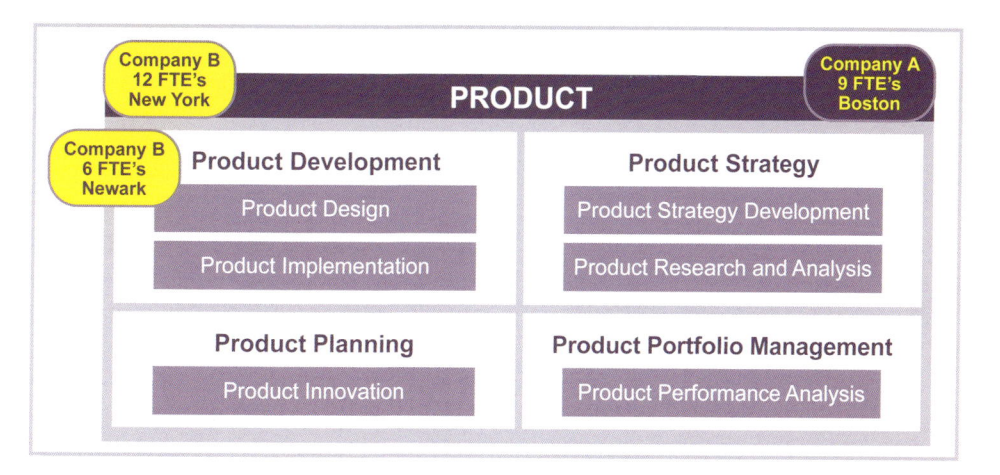

FIGURE 7-13: M&A Personnel Mapping.

Finally, mapping each organization's applications to a capability model can provide an easy visual to understand overlaps and gaps within the combined organization's systems architecture. Capturing company, system name, and a qualifier (e.g., line of business supported) can help you to quickly size up each organization's application assets and identify overlaps, redundancies, and gaps that may need to be addressed in the integration of the companies' technology domains. Figure 7-14 provides a visual example.

FIGURE 7-14: M&A Application Mapping.

Capability Model Uses–Conclusion

The examples provided in this book cover some of the many ways the ACORD Capability Model can be leveraged to support your business. Whether used as a foundational element of a holistic business architecture model, or for discrete activities to align people, process, and technology to a common business framework, the Capability Model can help you in your efforts to improve the effectiveness of your organization.

Parting Thoughts

The examples presented here are largely illustrative and straight-forward; implementers will find others. Use of the model will surface perspectives that serve to validate content and influence future iterations of the model via additional content.

Over time, the model will change (in fact, there are potential donations for new content happening as this book is going to print). As the model changes, ACORD will publish new editions of this book.

We hope you've enjoyed your journey through the pages of this text. If you want to learn more about the ACORD Capability Model, check out http://www.acord.org.